MORE
RANGERS GREATS

Teacher's award

This certificate is awarded to

Craig MacGregor

Class _____ P7

Signed _Miss Hutchison_   Date 1st Oct 1996.

MORE
RANGERS GREATS

Dixon Blackstock

Foreword by
John Greig, M.B.E.

SPORTSPRINT PUBLISHING
EDINBURGH

To Jean — for being another great

ISBN 0 85976 310 2

British Library Cataloguing in Publication Data
Blackstock, Dixon
  More Rangers greats.
  1. Scotland. Association football
  I. Title
  796.3340922

Acknowledgements

The author would like to thank all the great Rangers players who co-operated so fully in making the book possible. Also for the use of photographs from their own collection. Other picture thanks go to the *Sunday Mail, Sunday Post, Sun, Scotsman* Publications and D.C. Thomson.

Phototypeset by Beecee Typesetting Services
Printed in Great Britain by Billing & Sons Ltd, Worcester

surprised that Jimmy Millar was *Rangers Greats*.

his trade, I was fortunate enough
burgh every day with Jimmy and
ot from them on the field . . . but
carriage as they talked football to

nderestimated player. He made his
d. He could have played anywhere
of the game.
as best man at my wedding.
arity in football . . . a scoring winger.
ght balance to the tremendous team I
the 1960s. He was also a great striker of
ot.
tner Ronnie McKinnon was a colleague
n the reserves, through to the first team
onal football.
ouble centre half before the term was even
was quick, and a first-class reader of the

eat German Franz Beckenbauer telling our
ddell that he considered Ronnie to be one of
er seen.
unate enough to play with, and ultimately
ike Tom Forsyth and Davie Cooper.
y capacity as club Public Relations Officer, I
up of the new generation of players at Ibrox.
ad great success with the club; so has Richard
n a lot more to come.
lways been legends at Ibrox; and without doubt
on the horizon.

John Greig

Like Andy Cameron, I was
not included in the original
As a young player learning
to travel through from Edi
Ralphie Brand. I learned a
just as much in the railway
me.

Jimmy was always an
name as a centre-forwar
such was his knowledge
Jimmy, incidentally,
Davie Wilson was a r
He brought just the ri
played with at Ibrox in
the ball with either fo

My old sparring pa
right from our days i
and on into internati
We were playing d
thought of. Ronnie
game.

I can recall the g
manager Willie Wa
the best he had ev
I was also fort
manage, players
And now in m
can get a close-
Terry Butcher h
Gough and wit
There have a
there are more

m
Gr
Q
invo
books
all des
Perso
the decis
I am su
pleased as
When I w
footballer, p
were househo
many of the o
esteem.
They were the
time, and Rangers
tremendous years f
Rangers are dete
should never be forg
half a century after
Thornton is still on the

Contents

Foreword by John Greig   v

Acknowledgements   iv

1.   Introduction   1

2.   Willie Thornton   6

3.   Willie Woodburn   19

4.   Jimmy Millar   35

5.   Davie Wilson   49

6.   Ron McKinnon   62

7.   Tom Forsyth   80

8.   Davie Cooper   94

9.   Terry Butcher   110

10.   Richard Gough   129

Rangers Facts   146

CHAPTER 1

Introduction

MANY GREAT MEN AND GREAT PLAYERS HAVE influenced the direction taken by Rangers in the club's 118 years. But only a handful have shaped the destiny of the club: William Wilton at the turn of the century as the club's manager-secretary; his successor Bill Struth who dominated at Ibrox for 34 years. Scot Symon followed Struth and won six championships in 13 years and also led Rangers into the great new venture that was European football. Willie Waddell, a former hero on the field, returned to lay the foundations for the modern stadium which has made Ibrox the finest in the country.

They all have a vital place in the story and glory of Rangers. But there seems little doubt that when the time comes for some historians to put down the words tracing the club's progress in the second century of its existence . . . the name Graeme Souness will be writ large.

Souness has a long way to go yet to match the astounding roll of honours won by Struth — 18 championships and 10 Scottish Cups between 1920 and 1954. But he is catching up fast on Scot Symon's half-dozen titles.

However, the contribution to Rangers by Souness has gone far beyond the actual biff-and-bang purveyed on the pitch. Former Chairman David Holmes knew he was taking on a winner when he stunned Scottish football by recruiting Edinburgh-born Souness as player-manager from Italian club Sampdoria where the moustachioed Scot was strutting his stuff.

1

Holmes had been given the job of rousing the sleeping giant of Scottish football, as Rangers were being tagged at that time in 1986. The commission came from millionaire Lawrence Marlborough, who for some unknown reason preferred life in Lake Tahoe, Nevada to Copland Road, Govan.

Holmes had been trained as a joiner, but he knew a jewel when he saw one . . . even if it was a bit of a rough diamond! He will tell you that the first and the last name he thought of was Graeme Souness to replace Jock Wallace, another jaggy gem, but one who had lost the cutting edge. Souness had the credentials Holmes was seeking: experience, ambition and a will to win that had made him a lot of admirers and quite a few enemies (you could usually spot them because of the limp).

He had won everything with Liverpool; been capped more than 50 times by Scotland; and had gained valuable experience in Italy in two years with Sampdoria. The move worked with a success that was startling and swift. Souness didn't just jolt the giant that was dozing at Ibrox . . . he roused everything but the Loch Ness monster!

He went out and did what the detractors said you couldn't do: he bought success. As he poured millions into the transfer market — but also shrewdly brought millions back into the club by selling astutely — other clubs charged in behind him.

In no time Scottish football pitches were ringing with strange shouts in odd tongues. There was Olegs at Ibrox; Dareks at Parkhead; Lucs at Motherwell; Miodgrags at Tannadice; Hans at Pittodrie; Istvans at East End Park; Sergeis at St. Johnstone. Football's foreign legion had set up camp in Scotland . . . lured not by the Pied Piper but the pay packet. Players arrived and departed from Ibrox with the regularity of the Glasgow subway that passes almost under the stadium.

Winning the championship in his very first season was a bonus, but it didn't satisfy Souness. He was continually chopping and changing personnel in search of the perfect side. He plundered the English international side to bring Terry

Butcher, Chris Woods, Gary Stevens and Trevor Steven to Scotland. And he raided the English League scene to recruit Terry Hurlock, Nigel Spackman, Chris Vinnicombe and the richly talented Mark Walters who has the ability to be the most entertaining player in Scottish football one minute, and a pain in the tracksuit the next.

But his two boldest moves made the Rangers fans see red-heads. And some of them simply saw red. The signing of Maurice Johnston at Ibrox on July 10, 1989 was a unique transfer — it managed to upset almost as many Rangers fans as it did Celtic! Mo was not only a former Celtic player; he was a Catholic who had been ordered off in a Cup Final against Rangers and was seemingly destined for a return to Parkhead in a highly-publicised move from France where he had spent two years with Nantes.

Rangers will deny they hi-jacked Johnston. They simply saw an opportunity when it became clear that the deal involving Celtic was foundering and moved in quietly to haul Mo on board. There was indignation. Consternation. Resignation. Demonstration and scarve burning.

But Souness, the club and the player steered calmly through the storm, although Johnston at one point was surrounded by more minders than Madonna. Even now, two years, dozens of fine games and many goals later there are still those who mutter about betrayal. Mo must have been glad when big Mark Hateley was recruited from Monaco to share the burden. Not the goal burden. Mark became the No. 1 target for the jeer leaders . . . mainly because the Johnston-Hateley partnership brought an exclusion order for the highly popular Ally McCoist. Ally spent so long on the bench that the other players were nick-naming him 'The Judge'!

All the fuss . . . the fire . . . the fury from the fans scarcely moved Souness. He is nothing if not single-minded in his pursuit of success for Rangers. And he also appears to thrive on aggro. Since it is now missing from his life on the pitch, he creates it in the Press: League reconstruction, winter shut-

downs, hammer throwers in Scottish football . . . or another
S.F.A. blunder. Souness sails blithely from one storm to
another, either blissfully unaware of the boiling waters around
him or, more likely, totally unconcerned.

It has not all been a tale of unremitting triumph. Knee
injuries cost Rangers the services of the talented youngster Ian
Durrant and £1.4 million Soviet signing Oleg Kuznetsov, a red-
haired Russian giant who was meant to settle into the heart of
the defence but instead found himself bedded down in hospital
after just one-and-a-half games in Scottish football.

And the Scottish Cup proved to be a continual source of
irritation: defeat at the hands of Hamilton, Dunfermline and
Celtic (twice) was all Rangers had to show for the first four
seasons of trying under Souness. The 1-0 loss at Hampden in
the 1989-90 Final against Celtic at Hampden deprived Souness
of the opportunity to become the fourth Rangers manager to
achieve the triple crown. Bill Struth did it in 1948-49; Scot
Symon in 1963-64; and Jock Wallace managed it twice inside
three years: 1975-76 and 1977-78.

Rangers went into the game at Hampden on May 20,
strong favourites after winning the title in convincing style
three weeks earlier with a 4-0 home victory over Hearts at
Ibrox. They finished six points clear of Aberdeen. But
complacency is a fatal flaw in the make-up for an Old Firm
game; and a first-half mistake by right-back Gary Stevens let
Celtic's Joe Miller in for the only goal of the match.

New club chairman David Murray was philosophical:
'Rangers have a lot to look back on . . . but a lot more to look
forward to.' Millionaire Murray entered the frame at Ibrox on
November 23, 1988 . . . lured there by what he believed to be a
sound business investment as he paid out six million pounds to
buy out the Lawrence shares. But most of all he was drawn by
the persuasive talk of a close friend . . . Graeme Souness.

Souness was renowned as a midfield link man in his days
as a player: but he exceeded all previous efforts by linking
Murray to Ibrox. And after he had persuaded his boss to hire

him, he then bought a £600,000 stake in the business himself. Not so much a management buy-out as a manager buy-in.

Player, manager, director and major shareholder. Souness has already ensured a unique place for himself in Rangers' history.

And future matches will be played before 48,000 all-seated fans in the revamped Ibrox Stadium which is adding at least another £14 million to the building bill. Luxury executive boxes will extend out onto heated open-air verandahs and allow the lucky few to enjoy the atmosphere . . . but not the cold.

Changed times indeed from the humble beginnings when young men like the McNeil brothers, Moses and Peter, and their friends met on Glasgow Green to kick a ball around and decided to form a football team called Rangers. Stadiums costing £50 million pounds; players costing £2 million and earning wages of £5,000 a week. That was as likely as putting a man on the moon in those days. But 118 years on and, just like a man on the moon, it's a fact. Just like the 41 League championships; the 24 Scottish Cups; the 17 League Cups; and the 1972 European Cup Winners Cup.

And chairman Murray maintains there is more to look forward to: more great days for Rangers, and undoubtedly More Rangers Greats.

CHAPTER 2

Willie Thornton

THE OLD TIMERS IN THE WEST LOTHIAN MINING village of Winchburgh would always tell you that Jim was the REAL player in the footballing Thornton family. But it was his younger brother Willie who went on to footballing fame, if not fortune (no £5,000-a-week players in his time). Yet to this day, Willie admits that his big brother Jim was 'quite a player'.

He was also a bit of a hot-head and always in trouble with the referee . . . 'sent off quite a few times,' recalls Willie. Which makes the contrast in approach between the brothers even more startling. For in 18 years as a professional footballer, Willie Thornton was never ordered off . . . or booked . . . in fact, he was not even spoken to by a referee.

'Not my style', smiles Willlie, who at the age of 71, is still doing his bit for Rangers as custodian of the club's impressive trophy room and also acts as host at times in the hospitality suite named after him in the heart of the main stand.

What was the Thornton style was an inbuilt radar which let him home in with perfect timing on a cross ball . . . usually sent over at the end of a typical thundering run by his team-mate and friend Willie Waddell.

But there was more to Willie Thornton than a good head. Inside that famous napper was a shrewd football brain. He was a student of the game who read play well, knew the strengths and weaknesses of the opposition. He could feed the ball off to his team-mates with considerable skill.

6

In his prime . . . Willie Thornton in the days when he was Ibrox top scorer four seasons in succession.

But even Willie was startled by the description of him in a handsome, informative production titled *Glasgow Rangers — Player by Player*. 'The author kindly bestowed on me "a silky touch as a left sided player with a deft touch in his left foot". I don't think I used my left foot for much more than standing on. But I'm flattered all the same by the description.'

Opponents who faced Thornton in his days as a teenager before the War, and as a seasoned ex-soldier afterwards, must have been quite happy he didn't possess the extra qualities ascribed to him.

He was more than enough to handle as it was. Right from his debut as a 16-year-old at outside-right against Partick Thistle, Rangers knew they had a rare talent. 'Not as an outside-right, mind you,' says Willie. 'I was always a centre-forward. I suppose I was played on the wing just to break me in gently.' That debut day was January 2, 1937 at Firhill, and he went on to play half-a-dozen times in that first season.

That he ever arrived at Ibrox at all was due to the combined efforts of his brother Jim and a proud uncle. But not Willie's uncle. The man in question was secretary of Winchburgh Albion, the local team for which the Thorntons played. He had a nephew playing at inside-right, and wrote to Rangers inviting them to come and look at him. Which they did. But it was the young centre-forward who caught the eye of scout Alec Young, who promptly had the 15-year-old Willie Thornton out on trial in a reserve game against Kilmarnock. He scored two goals that afteroon, and went back to Winchburgh . . . to find a Hearts scout in the Thornton home inviting him to Tynecastle to meet the manager.

Enter brother Jim. He was a Rangers fan, and promptly got the local club secretary to phone Bill Struth that very Saturday night. The result was that the next day, Sunday, March 7th 1936 . . . just four days after his 16th birthday . . . Willie Thornton signed for Rangers at Ibrox. 'I was still at school, so the form was put away in a drawer until I could officially join them,' recalls Willie. 'And I was taken on at £1 a week.'

That sum was doubled on his debut day. Not for the first time the legendary Bill Struth was to show his amazing capacity for winning the hearts and minds of his players. As Thornton prepared for his big day, manager Struth asked him: 'How much am I paying you, boy?' When he was told £1 he replied: 'Anyone who keeps his boots as clean as you deserves double

A trophy-room reunion. Willie Thornton happily displays the Scottish Cup flanked by former Ibrox hero Bob McPhail (right) and another ex-Ranger . . . Egyptian Mohamed Latif who played with the club in the years before the Second World War.

that.' Which sent the teenage Thornton out in jubilant mood. And sure as fate his wage packet next week contained £2.

'He was an incredible man,' recalls Thornton. 'He instinctively knew how to get the best out of people. He was like a second father to young players and influenced and helped shape the lives of so many of us. You never wanted to let him down. He convinced us for years that we were better than any other side. And we believed him. We stepped out on the pitch week after week absolutely sure of our own superiority.'

The teenage Thornton was edging out an Ibrox legend in the latter years of the 1930s. And there could hardly be a more striking contrast between the slight, 5ft 8in figure of the boy Thornton and the huge intimidating presence of big Jimmy Smith. Smith, later to become trainer at Ibrox, was undoubtedly a better player than his reputation allowed. But his name was built round his physical prowess, and in the days when goalkeepers were left to fend for themselves, there was nothing Smith enjoyed more than dumping an unprepared keeper into the back of the net. He scored more than 300 League and Cup goals for Rangers, so it was little wonder some fans looked upon the slight frame of Thornton with reservations.

But even the doubters began to warm to the youngster as in his second season he played in 20 matches and scored seven goals. 'It was unbelievable,' says Willie. 'Just three years earlier I had nipped away from school at Broxburn to sit on the touchline at a Hearts-Rangers Scottish Cup replay at Tynecastle on a Wednesday afternoon. Now I found myself playing with nine or 10 of the same Rangers players. It was stuff straight from the comic books.'

Willie acknowledges the help given to him in those teenage times by legends like Davie Meiklejohn and Bob McPhail. 'Davie was in the reserves when I was breaking through, and it was his recommendation that got me my first-team place. He was Bill Struth's right-hand man. And when I did get in the team, Bob McPhail counselled and advised me all the way.'

But Willie also remembers when the same McPhail was less than chuffed with his young prodigy. 'I used to travel on the train every day from Linlithgow, and would get in the compartment beside Alex Venters who was coming through from Fife. Alex and I struck up a good partnership and were scoring a lot of goals. He used to tell me all the time as we travelled that all I had to do was get the ball, and feed it to him at inside-right. This I was doing dutifully, and as I say it was bringing goals. I scored 23 in season 1938-39.'

But his slavish adherence to the words of Venters brought a sharp reminder from McPhail at the interval in one game. As they left the field, big Bob called the teenager to his side. 'I thought I was going to get some more advice,' says Willie. Instead what he heard was: 'Here you, do you know you have a f------ inside left playing with you?' Willie might have been a

Old pals act . . . the formidable duo of Willie Thornton and Willie Waddell, two men who between them scored nearly 250 goals for Rangers

boy, but he wasn't a daft lad and was shrewd enough to heed the message and spread his favours round after that.

He was still a teenager when he won his first League championship medal in 1938-39 as Rangers scored 112 goals in gathering up 59 points . . . 11 ahead of second-placed Celtic. Willie had the soccer world at his feet. But not long after that, the only thing at his feet turned out to be army issue boots. Five League games, and a Glasgow Cup tie into season 1939-40 . . . and War was declared. Young Thornton had already scored seven times in those few matches, which meant Rangers were once again leading . . . and Thornton seemed to be heading for the top.

Instead he found himself heading for places like Cairo, Tripoli, Anzio and Monte Cassino. And instead of the Light Blue of Rangers he was in the colours of the Scottish Horse Regiment, which was founded by the Duke of Atholl.

He almost got his first cap before going into uniform as a 20-year-old in April 1940. He was due to play against England at Hampden . . . but was injured in a midweek match anyway and ruled out. The next action he was to see was as a guest player with Norwich where he scored two goals in five games before Gunner William Thornton, wireless operator, was posted overseas. It was 1946 before he swopped army brown for Ibrox blue again. In between times he was involved in the hard slog of army work in Egypt and Tripoli and involved in three landings in Italy.

And it was during one such operation that Gunner William Thornton won the second medal of his life . . . this time the highly meritorious Military Medal for his actions in Sicily on November 18, 1943. 'Just doing my job,' is how Willie sums it up. But when he was to return to play in his first Old Firm game three years later, he received a standing ovation from both Rangers and Celtic supporters for a job well done.

There WAS some football in the midst of the war action. 'We used to play regimental games near Anzio. There were no lines around the pitch — only trenches,' recalls Willie. 'They came in handy at times. The Germans had a big gun we called Anzio Archie. You could hear it being fired from miles away. Whenever it popped, we knew we had time to hit the trenches before it landed.'

There was also a Central Mediterranean side which featured other stars in uniform like Tom Finney of Preston and George Hamilton of Aberdeen. 'I can remember we played a big game in Rimini, and before the match the Sappers were on the field checking it for mines. They used lines of tape up the middle to show where they had been working and I said to George Hamilton: "I'll be going down those marked zones. Don't bother sending the ball to the wings".' This must have been the forerunner of the 'channels of play' so beloved of modern coaches.

'The war took six years out of my footballing life. But that was no price to pay, considering what it did to many other people's lives,' says Willie. Incidentally, throughout the War while he was on active service Bill Struth made sure that his mother was paid £2 a week by Rangers. 'Just another example of his shrewdness, and also his kindness,' says Willie.

GNR. William Thornton
-Royal Regiment of Artillery 1939-45-
(80th Scottish Horse)
(Duke of Atholl)

BUCKINGHAM PALACE.

I greatly regret that I am
unable to give you personally the
award which you have so well earned.
I now send it to you with
my congratulations and my best
wishes for your future happiness.

George R.I.

986279 Gnr. W. Thornton, R.A.
Royal Regiment of Artillery.

CITATION
BUCKINGHAM PALACE
H.R.H. King George VI

MILITARY MEDAL
Awarded in the Field
- Sicily Italy -
18th. November 1943

The most treasured of the Thornton medal collection . . . The Military Medal Gunner William Thornton won for valour in the field in Sicily in 1943.

When he returned to play for Rangers in 1946 he had spent the past few months working as a physical training instructor in Venice and was fit enough to be pitched into first-team football. And promptly picked up where he left off . . . sticking the ball into the net.

Season 1946-47 opened up for Rangers with a League game against Motherwell at Fir Park. Thornton scored the first goal as Rangers went on to a 4-2 victory. The teams that day on August 10 were:

Motherwell: Johnston; Kilmarnock, Shaw; McLeod, Paton, Russell; Henderson, Redpath, Brown, Bremner, Barclay.

Rangers: Brown; Cox, Shaw; Watkins, Young, Symon; Waddell, Gillick, Thornton, Duncanson, Caskie.

It was certainly a hot August month for Thornton who

scored two hat-tricks in succession against Falkirk and Third Lanark. When the season ended 29 games later, Rangers were champions for the 25th time, taking the title by two points from Hibs. They scored 76 goals, with 19 of them coming from top scorer Thornton. And there was the first of two successive League Cup medals as Rangers beat Aberdeen 4-0 at Hampden, with Thornton having scored six goals in that competition as well.

In that post-war period, the people of Britain went crazy over football . . . 'a kind of mass hysteria,' says Willie. Huge crowds flocked to big matches. And to watch teams packed with quality players. 'I think we had the near perfect team,' says Willie. 'But we had to play to our best every week. There were so many good players at other clubs you couldn't be complacent. But we were confident. Struth had instilled that in us. We felt fitter, stronger than the rest. And the side was full of strong characters.

'I can't recall any of the Iron Curtain team as it came to be called ever asking away from Ibrox.' What he can recall is the routine that would make most managers, and certainly the pampered stars of today, blanche. 'Bill Struth hated cars. He wouldn't let the players travel to training in them. He had a flat right at the corner of Copland Road and used to watch for the players arriving by underground or bus. If he was suspicious, he would send the doorman round the streets in the district to check to see if there were any players' cars parked nearby. When you got in to the ground, you went straight out on the track in the clothes you arrived in and did a few brisk walking laps of the stadium. Then it was in to change and start the real training.'

And every week there was the routine called 'getting your medicine'. 'I think the boss believed that players would go out every weekend and have a right good time to themselves. So he believed in "clearing you out". That involved a dose of laxative . . . either castor oil, liquid paraffin or black draught, which was liquorice-based. I'll tell you, there was many a hasty exit from the subway on the way back from training!'

Because of his P.T.I. experience at the end of the war, Willie wanted to go to Jordanhill College for a year to become a gym teacher. 'Bill Struth didn't facy that. He didn't want his players to have anything to do with Jordanhill. During the War I had written a lot to him, and he told me he had shown the letters to a friend of his in newspapers and advised me to go see him.'

And that's how Willie started a career in a local Glasgow evening paper as a sub-editor. 'After I was trained, I used to go into work in Hope Street, Glasgow, an hour early, leave at 9.30 to go to Ibrox for training and be back at my desk after 12 without ever taking a lunch break. Guys like Sammy Cox used to give me some stick. "I'm off to Ayr races, and you're away to work", he would laugh. But I enjoyed combining the jobs.'

And it certainly never got in the way of goals. He scored 21 League, League Cup and Scottish Cup goals in season 1947-48, winning his first Scottish Cup medal in the process. It came in a replayed Final against Morton after a 1-1 draw. The two games drew crowds of 131,975 and 129,176. And previously the semi-final against Hibs had drawn an astonishing 143,570, which still stands as a semi record. Which brings a grand total of 404,721!

'That Final is one of my greatest memories,' says Willie. 'I desperately wanted a Cup medal. But after the draw in the first meeting with Morton, I was summoned up to Bill Struth's room. I was stunned when he told me he was thinking of playing Billy Williamson at centre-forward in the replay and what did I think. I didn't know what to say. Then he told me I would be playing at inside-right and I said I thought it was a great idea . . . I was so relieved to be still playing I would have turned out at centre-half.'

Struth, for the umpteenth time, turned out to have played a trump card. The only goal of the Final came with just four minutes left of extra time . . . a bulleted header by Williamson. His only goal in his only Cup appearance that year. The teams were:

Rangers: Brown; Young, Shaw; McColl, Woodburn, Cox; Rutherford, Thornton, Williamson, Duncanson, Gillick.
Morton: Cowan; Mitchell, Whigham; Campbell, Millar, Whyte; Hepburn, Murphy, Cupples, Orr, Liddell.

Willie may have lost valuable time in the forces: but he was wasting no time in making up for this. His medal collection rose by THREE in 1948-49 as Rangers swept to a tremendous treble. They won the League by a point from Dundee . . . who needed victory in the last game of the season against Falkirk at Brockville but crashed 4-1. They beat Celtic 2-1 in the Final of the League Cup before 105,000 fans at Hampden and took the Scottish Cup with a 4-1 win over Clyde. In the process, Thornton scored 34 goals, including a hat-trick in the last League game against Albion Rovers at Coatbridge which ensured the championship.

He picked up the last of his medals in season 1949-50: his fourth League badge and a Scottish Cup medal that was all the sweeter since he not only scored his only Scottish Cup goals of the season . . . but also his only goals in a major Hampden Final. He scored with two flashing headers inside two minutes in the second half to tie up a 3-0 victory over East Fife before a 120,015 crowd. Willie Findlay had opened the scoring after just 30 seconds. The teams were:
Rangers: Brown; Young, Shaw; McColl, Woodburn, Cox; Rutherford, Findlay, Thornton, Duncanson, Rae.
East Fife: Easson; Laird, Stewart; Philp, Finlay, Aitken; Black, Fleming, Morris, Brown, Duncan.

The next few seasons continued to bring goals from Willie: but no more glittering prizes. And despite his score rate for Rangers, he won scant international honours for a man of his prowess . . . just seven full caps. 'But I did play against all the Home Countries,' he points out. He scored in only one of his Scotland matches, against Denmark in Copenhagen in May 1952.

'But there was one special international for me,' says Willie. 'We might have lost 2-0 to England at Hampden in

No way through. This time Willie Thornton is frustrated by Dundee goalkeeper Bill Brown in the 1951 League Cup Final at Hampden which Rangers lost 3-2.

1948. But I had the privilege of shaking hands with one of my War-time heroes, Field Marshall Montgomery, in the pre-match introductions. That meant a lot to me.' And you can be sure Monty was pleased to meet ex-Gunner Thornton, M.M.

Willie left Rangers after season 1953-54 . . . only playing eight games but managing seven goals. He was Scotland's Player of the Year in 1952. He played 303 major games for Rangers and scored 188 goals. Fourteen years later he was back at Ibrox as assistant manager to Davie White.

Between times he had spent six years as manager of Dundee, where he recruited a rich source of talent for the club including Ian Ure, Alan Gilzean, Jim Gabriel, Andy Penman, Hugh Robertson, Alan Cousin and Alex Hamilton . . . some of whom were sold for high prices.

Then followed eight years at Firhill as boss in succession to one of his boyhood heroes Davie Meiklejohn. But when the call came to return to Rangers, he didn't hesitate. Fifty-five years after he first walked up them, the marble steps at Ibrox remain the magic stairway for Willie Thornton.

Willie Thornton's honours:

1946

Oct.	Wales	(a)	1-3
Nov.	Northern Ireland	(h)	0-0

1947

Oct.	Northern Ireland	(a)	0-2

1948

Apr.	England	(h)	0-2

1949

Apr.	France	(h)	2-0

1952

May	Denmark	(a)	2-1
May	Sweden	(a)	1-3

CHAPTER 3

Willie Woodburn

THOUSANDS OF SCOTS REMEMBER WILLIE Woodburn for what he was . . . probably the finest centre-half the country ever produced.

Unfortunately, thousands of others remember him only for what he became . . . the first and only MAJOR Scottish football star to be handed down the shameful sentence of a *sine die* suspension.

Even today, 37 years on, that decision by the Scottish Football Association still hurts the man who was known to millions as 'Big Ben'. Woodburn was 34 and near the end of his career anyway when he was ordered off for the fifth time in his 16-year career. He knew he was in for a hard sentence when he went up before the S.F.A. on September 14, 1954.

'But I never dreamed I would be banned for life' says Willie, who is now in his 70s but retains that lean, hard frame which made him such a formidable defender. 'I deserved to be punished. I admit that. But I was near the end of my career anyway. I had been sent off just five times in 17 seasons.

'And I had played for Scotland 24 times. I was expecting a stiff sentence. But even to this day I cannot believe that the men who sat in judgement that day couldn't have looked at the situation clearly and simply suspended me say for six months. At that stage and age it would have probably meant the end of my career anyway. And it would have given me the chance to retire with dignity. I don't think that was too much to ask.'

The judgement is hard to comprehend nowadays in an era

19

where there are players who have records far worse than Woodburn . . . some have ordering-off totals running well into double figures. Also nowadays, the ruling bodies are very much aware of the legal consequences of denying a player the right to earn his living. Even then, back in 1954, Woodburn and the Players Union sought counsel's advice and could easily have challenged the ban.

'But I decided against it. I had too much respect for the game and I didn't want the law to become involved in football.'

So Woodburn suffered in silence. And the fact that the ban was lifted two years later is fully indicative of the belief that, inside football, it was regarded as an extreme action which should never have been taken. It was too late for Woodburn to resume his career. He was, anyway, a partner with his brother in a thriving car business in Edinburgh, and had started writing about football for the *News of the World*.

'It's a stain that will never be removed,' says Willie sadly. But he is not hypocritical about the action which led to his life ban. A quiet, pleasant man off the field, he was always a ferocious competitor on the pitch. And possessor of a fiery temper which reached blow-out point quickly.

His long-time colleague Bobby Brown, who played in goal behind Woodburn for many years just after the second war, recalls that usually Big Ben was in trouble for going to protect other players whom he believed were being hard done to by the opposition.

'We used to keep an eye on Willie. The danger sign was when he started pulling angrily at the chest of his jersey, as though he was making room for some drastic action. One of us would always get to him quickly at that point and calm him down.'

But there was no-one on the scene quickly enough that fateful Saturday afternoon at Ibrox when Rangers met Stirling Albion in a League Cup tie on August 28, 1954. Ironically, there was less than a minute to go and Rangers were leading 2-0 thanks to goals in the 85th and 87th minutes from Paton and

The craggy features of Willie Woodburn in the 1940s.

Hubbard, when Woodburn and Stirling striker Paterson went in for a tackle.

Willie recalls the moment as though it were yesterday instead of 36 years in the past. 'I tackled him hard but fair. But our legs got in a tangle, and he twisted my leg badly. In a reaction to the pain I made the biggest mistake of my life. If I had punched him, I might even have got away with it as simply just a rush of blood.'

But this time Woodburn not only lost the head . . . he used it. 'It was an action that haunts me to this day,' he says. 'I will never understand why I did it. I will regret those few seconds all the days of my life'. Typically Willie adds: 'I have never held anything against Paterson since. I was the one who lost the place. But, do you know all the men I "killed" were all able to play the next game. I hurt myself more than them.'

It was a sad end to a distinguished career which had begun in the late 1930s when Woodburn, a product of the rugby-playing Heriot's school in Edinburgh, ignored the pleas of his English teacher and gave up rugby for football.

The tall, skinny youngster who started playing at wing half for Edinburgh Ashton juvenile side before settling in at centre-half, was expected to sign for Hearts. Not only were the family all Tynecastle supporters, Willie was born in a top floor tenement at 164 Gorgie Road, a throw-in away from the Hearts ground. 'But I got fed up waiting for Hearts, and when the chance came to join Rangers I jumped at it,' says Willie.

But he thought he had blown his future before it even started when he played a trial game against Queen's Park at Ibrox. 'The trainer Arthur Dixon came to me and said the boss wanted to see me upstairs. I had just given away a penalty in the game, and quite honestly I thought that was me out the window. But the first words Bill Struth ever spoke to me were: "How do you like being a Rangers player?" I blurted out an apology for the penalty. And all he said was, "The man who never made a mistake, never made anything." And that was me a Rangers player.'

The teenage Woodburn was working as an apprentice plasterer in those days, and was ordered to serve out his time by Struth. He was also staying in digs in Glasgow. And if he wasn't in bed by 10 p.m., the landlady was on the phone to Struth the next day. 'It was a bit like the army under old Bill,' reflects Woodburn. 'All that hard work and discipline for £4 a week, too.'

Woodburn was always noted as a two-footed player, which came from hard work, not natural ability. 'Old Arthur Dixon had me banging away against a wall with both feet. I

Woodburn displays the fierce concentration which made him such a formidable defender.

used to wear a rubber shoe on my right foot and a boot on my left just to make sure I kept on working it.'

Woodburn was 19 when he made his first-team debut in season 1938-39. 'I was lucky,' says Willie. 'I stepped into the team just as Jimmy Simpson, who was the father of goalkeeper Ronnie, was finishing his long career.' But it didn't take long for people to realise that in Woodburn Rangers had found another defender of outstanding ability!

He played 13 League games towards the end of his first season as Rangers took the title outright for the 23rd time. And he made the No. 5 spot his own as Scottish football headed into what looked like being a tremendous season for the teenage Woodburn in 1938-39. This prospect seemed even brighter as Rangers opened up with a 5-1 victory over St. Mirren at Ibrox . . . with a certain W. Woodburn on the score-sheet.

Four games later Rangers were still unbeaten and at the top of the table. But the day after their 2-1 win over Third Lanark at Cathkin on September 2, 1939 a former Austrian house painter ensured that an ex-Edinburgh plasterer was not going to kick a ball that counted for six years. I was going to say 'kick a ball in anger', but Willie being Willie, that hardly seems the right phrase.

Wartime football, with its regional and then Southern League title, brought visiting big-name stars to Scottish football to play as guests for various teams. But it held no great appeal to Woodburn. Less so when in September 1942 he badly damaged his cartilage in a game against Hibs at Easter Road. Mind you, considering the score line, it's harder to say what hurt more . . . his knee or his pride. Hibs walloped Rangers 8-1, with Bobby Combe scoring four of the goals!

'Being a Rangers man living in Edinburgh was bad enough. But with a Hearts background as well, I took some fearful ribbing after that game,' recalls Willie.

Making matters even worse, by the time Woodburn recovered several months later, big George Young had been established in the centre-half berth. It was to take Woodburn until September 28, 1946 to shift big Corky over. He replaced the injured Young in a League Cup tie against Queen's Park at Hampden and never looked back.

The teams that day were:

Queen's Park: G. Hamilton; J. Mitchell, W. Johnstone; D. Letham, J. Whigham, I. Harnett; A. Aitken, A. McAulay, C. Liddell, H. Millar, I. Irvine.

Rangers: Brown; Gray, Shaw; Cox, Woodburn, Symon; Waddell, Gillick, Thornton, Duncanson, Caskie.

A summer-time pose from Woodburn in one of Rangers alternative strips.

Duncanson with a double, Gillick and Thornton got the Rangers goals with Aitken and Liddell scoring for Queen's.

Woodburn had missed the first nine League games, but played in 18 of the next 21 as Rangers picked up where they left off before they were so rudely interrupted . . . as champions.

And with the League Cup won as well, by 4-0 over Aberdeen at Hampden, it was a happy return to first-team duty for Big Ben.

Incidentally, he didn't have that nickname at that point in time. And as it turns out, when he did get tagged it was nothing to do with the fact that he struck with the same heavy clang as the famous clock at the Houses of Parliament.

'I got the name after manager Bill Struth took us to Portugal to play a team called Benfica in a friendly. We beat them 3-0, and at the celebration party afterwards I grabbed the microphone and put on such a performance I was immediately christened Ben'.

That trip incidentally was made by Dakota aircraft of the now defunct Scottish Airways . . . and set the trend of future trips abroad. In the past it had always been leisurely boat voyages.

By 1947 Rangers were about to enter a new era . . . the iron curtain years were about to drop on Scottish football. It would appear that the first time the legendary curtain was lowered was in a League Cup tie at Ibrox against Third Lanark.

For the first time the defence read: Brown; Young, Shaw; McColl, Woodburn, Cox. Naturally, they didn't concede a goal. 'But I always felt that too much emphasis was placed on the defence,' says Woodburn. 'Not enough praise went the way of midfield men like Torry Gillick and Jimmy Duncanson . . . or the way Willie Waddell and Willie Thornton could get goal after goal'.

But it was that defence which won trophies for Rangers . . . and the statistics prove it. Hibs, when the Famous Five attack came into being, could always score more goals than Rangers. And could invariably do well against the Ibrox men themselves. But Hibs never had the same scrooge-like defence, and so in the early days of the iron curtain regime, Hibs had the flair but Rangers usually had the final say.

Not always, mind you. After Rangers took the title in 1946-47 by two points from their Edinburgh rivals, Hibs reversed the roles the following season to be champions by the

Eyes down . . . but not a full house this time. The terracings are empty as Willie poses for an action shot.

same margin. However, there was nothing Hibs or anyone else for that matter could do about season 1948-49 when Rangers swept all three major trophies away. The title was theirs by a point from Dundee, won by virtue of the fact that the Ibrox men lost only four games in the season to five by Dundee, who scored eight goals more than Rangers, but conceded 48 to their rivals' 32.

And Woodburn added two more medals to his collection as Rangers first of all defeated Raith Rovers 2-0 at Hampden in the League Cup Final before a 57,450 crowd, then a few months later disposed of Clyde 4-1 watched by 120,162 Scottish Cup Final fans.

'There were great players in almost every team in those days,' recalls Willie. 'And the crowds were fantastic. People were just desperate to see real action on the field again after the war years.'

But despite the huge attendances, wages were not extravagant. 'I think I finished up on £14 a week, plus £2 for a win and £1 for a draw. There were bonuses, of course, for Cup success, but they were never huge.' In fact, it's said that Lawrie Reilly, who had some tempestuous clashes with Big Ben, used to tease him during a game by telling him Hibs were on £100 a man for victory.

'He was a torment, Reilly. But a real good player,' says Willie. 'We had some fierce clashes, but always finished with a handshake.' In fact, Woody had so much respect for his Scotland international colleague that when Reilly was in dispute with Hibs at one point and refused to re-sign unless he got a testimonial, Woodburn and other Ibrox players tried to talk the club into signing him when Hibs put him on the transfer list.

The rivalry with Hibs continued in '49-50. Again Rangers won the flag by a point, with the Edinburgh side second. Again Hibs scored 86 goals to Rangers' 58. Again it was the defence that did the trick for the Ibrox men. They lost only two games and conceded just 26 goals. Hibs, beaten only three times,

No way past . . . Woodburn comes in the style that won a thousand tackles.

conceded 34 goals. They were still in with a chance of over-taking their rivals when they came to Ibrox on April 19 level on points.

But in a titanic battle, watched by an amazing 101,000 fans at Ibrox, Woodburn stood like a giant to turn away all that Smith, Johnstone, Reilly, Turnbull and Ormond could throw at him. 'We finished drawing 0-0 and we went on to draw our last game against Third Lanark and take the title,' recalls Willie. 'Mind you, Thirds gave us a fright. We were 2-0 up early on and coasting but wee Jimmy Mason got them back in the game and then Henderson missed a penalty before Cuthbertson got the equaliser.'

Perhaps the most frustrating chapter of all in the days of The Curtain v The Class came in 1952-53 when Hibs, champions for the past two seasons, were pipped by a decimal point for a hat-trick of titles. It was, of course, Rangers who did it. Or to be more precise, it would seem the defence again, since both teams finished on 43 points with Hibs once more out in front in goals for by 93 to 80 but Rangers taking the flag by virtue of conceding 39 goals to 51. 'We took the title by something like .227 on goal difference,' says Willie. 'But really, I would say that it was Willie Waddell who did the job. We needed a draw in the last game of the season against Queen of the South at Palmerston and were a goal down with just 15 minutes to go when "Deedle" drove through in that rampaging style of his and blasted in a beauty.'

Woodburn, of course, was not just a hero with Rangers. He was a key man for Scotland as well. But, incredibly, he was 28 before he won his first cap . . . against England at Wembley in 1947. And he crammed another 23 full honours into the last few years of his career, his last game being the 6-0 drubbing of the U.S.A. at Hampden on April 30, 1952 with his old pal Reilly hitting a hat-trick.

'I loved the games against England. Particularly at Wembley,' says Willie. 'I played there in '47, '49 and '51 and we drew the first of those games and won the other two. But oddly enough I also played against England at Hampden twice and finished up on the losing side both times.

'Stanley Matthews was a phenomenal player. Virtually unstoppable once he had the ball. So our plan always was to cut off the supply to him. Sometimes it worked, like in 1949 when Billy Steel did a fantastic job at inside forward for us, and, of course, Jimmy Cowan was unbelievable in goal as we won 3-1.'

Woodburn, like so many of his time, watches and wonders now at the wages and equipment available to the modern

Woodburn was not just a big strong defender . . . he had a lot of skill and control as he shows here shielding the ball from a challenge.

player. 'I used to have to take three weeks to break in a pair of boots,' recalls Willie. 'And it would only take three minutes to break your skull on a wet Saturday when the leather ball came plunging out of the air. It was like heading a curling stone.

'The players nowadays are lucky. But they are also talented. Willie Miller was a superb defender, with great timing. Craig Levein will get better and better. But I must say the money bothers me. When I was earning £14 a week, a good tradesman could make £8 or £9. So we weren't so far away from the punters. I just don't think the fans can relate to someone who is earning £5,000 a week.'

Big Ben in full flight. And, as in most games, it is hard to tell if he is jubilant or otherwise.

In his 17 years at Ibrox Woodburn played in four championship-winning teams; he won four Scottish Cup medals and two League Cup medals. His career total of games for Rangers totalled just one short of the 500.

Yet he will be remembered most for that one moment of indiscretion. The late Charlie Tully of Celtic, who described Woodburn as his favourite Scottish player, commented: 'He was hard but he was never dirty. In my opinion, the *sine die* suspension was harsh treatment for a man who served his country so well. He was one of the greatest Scots ever to wear the dark blue.'

Woodburn can take comfort from the fact that this view is widely shared . . . even by colleagues who risked injury sharing the Press Box with him in his writing career. Willie still had a habit of lashing out to clear every ball upfield, and a few journalists carried the bruises to prove it. In fact, at times you had to hang on to his jacket in the lofty eyries of Hampden, Ibrox and Parkhead to stop him taking off out the window going for a high ball!

Willie is retired now, living quietly in his fine bungalow home in Edinburgh with his wife Jane. The legacy of too many knee knocks has left him now in his 70s deprived of his other favourite sport . . . a game of golf. As someone who played with Willie at a few Football Writers' outings, I have to report that even on the fairways he was a man of marked impatience. You had to keep an eye out for the odd flying club.

Finally, just a word of warning to Scotland's football bosses. Willie's three daughters all married Englishmen — 'I think it was revenge for those Wembley games,' he jokes — so somewhere down south there might be a new Willie Woodburn hiding under an assumed name.

That will have to be watched. We simply can't have a descendant of Big Ben clocking on for England!

The Woodburn honours list:

1947

April	England	(a)	1-1
May	Belgium	(a)	1-2
May	Luxembourg	(a)	6-0
Oct.	Northern Ireland	(a)	0-2
Nov.	Wales	(h)	1-2

1949

April	England	(a)	3-1
April	France	(h)	2-0
Oct.	Northern Ireland	(a)	8-2
Nov.	Wales	(h)	2-0

1950

April	England	(h)	0-1
May	Portugal	(a)	2-2
May	France	(a)	1-0
Oct.	Wales	(a)	3-1
Nov.	Northern Ireland	(h)	6-1
Dec.	Austria	(h)	0-1

1951

April	England	(a)	3-2
May	Denmark	(h)	3-1
May	France	(h)	1-0
May	Belgium	(a)	5-0
May	Austria	(a)	0-4
Oct.	Northern Ireland	(a)	3-0
Nov.	Wales	(h)	0-1

1952

April	England	(h)	1-2
April	U.S.A.	(h)	6-0

CHAPTER 4

Jimmy Millar

THIS BOOK IS GUARANTEED AT LEAST ONE satisfied customer — Scots comedian Andy Cameron. The comic, an avid Ibrox fan, gave me bear's abuse for not including Jimmy Millar in the first series of *Rangers Greats*.

'The Old Warhorse' is how Andy described Millar . . . a man whom he described as 'epitomising everything a Ranger should be'. As it turns out, Andy is not alone in his views on Millar. Other Ibrox players from the Millar days are equally fulsome in their praise.

'Jim Baxter, Ian McMillan and others . . . they had tremendous skill, but lacked other qualities. Jimmy Millar had the lot. Ability and bravery in equal measures. Plus a football brain that was a lot more shrewd than he was ever given credit for.' Those are the words of another player featured in this book: Davie Wilson.

And yet another ex-Ibrox man Alex Willoughby simply says: 'Millar was the best of the lot. Even when he was having a bad game himself, he would make sure that others played well. He was always willing to take the pressure off the young guys around him.'

Jimmy Millar was probably what they call nowadays a player's player: a man whose qualities are known and respected by his team-mates but tend not to be recognised by the public. 'That kind of public recognition never bothered me,' says Jimmy. 'Basically I was always a shy kind of person. I wouldn't put myself forward.' Even today he is still having trouble getting recognised: the sign above the door of his pub in Leith says: Proprietor, J. Miller. 'The brewers put the sign up with the wrong spelling, he says. 'I must get it changed some day.'

The walls of the Duke's Head would tell the casual customer that this was a sporting pub. Football and golf pictures abound. But pride of place is not given to Jimmy Millar: the centrepiece belongs to the late, great Hearts centre Willie Bauld. 'He was my hero,' says Jimmy. 'What else would you expect from a boy from Dumbiedykes, which is Edinburgh's equivalent of the famous Glasgow Gorbals.'

But like so many Edinburgh youngsters in the years after the war, it was not Tynecastle where his destiny lay: he answered the familiar command of 'go West, young man' to join Rangers.

But there were a couple of wee diversions via Dunfermline and Cyprus first of all. Jimmy Millar was a 17-year-old apprentice plumber when he signed for Dunfermline from Merchiston Thistle. And it didn't take then Dunfermline manager Bobby Ancell long to recognise the ability of the young man from Edinburgh. But what he couldn't work out was just where to put the talents to best use. 'I was pitched into the first team more or less straight away,' says Jimmy. 'But it was at full back . . . inside right or inside left. Never centre-forward. As a matter of fact, centre-half was probably my best position. But I was just too wee at 5ft 9in.'

There is no doubt that in the modern game, Millar would have slotted neatly into the role of sweeper. He could tackle, was powerful in the air for his size, passed well and read the game with intelligence. It wasn't until season 1954-55 began that Millar took the first step on the journey which was to take him to Ibrox. 'Bobby Ancell came in at the start of the season and asked me if I fancied playing centre-forward. I said sure. Between the August and the January I rattled in 20 goals. That's when Rangers came for me.'

Millar has fond memories of his Dunfermline days. 'A

Now hear this. Jimmy Millar gets an earful from famous referee Tiny Wharton.

great place to learn, even though it was in the Second Division. I played against great names like Willie Redpath of Motherwell and Morton's goalkeeper Jimmy Cowan. He was so wee you wonder how he got picked for Scotland.'

The Fifers didn't have a lot of money, but there were some unexpected bonuses, as Jimmy recalls: 'We beat Stenhousemuir in an important game, and the directors were very pleased. One of them was a local butcher. And the next Tuesday night when we came in for training, there was a wee parcel hanging on every player's hook. It was 2lbs of tripe each!'

When Rangers came in for Millar on January 12th, 1955 his 'bonus' was a wee bit more substantial . . . 'but not by a lot,' he says. 'The fee was around £5,000 . . . and I was given a £20 signing-on fee. I can recall to this day Scot Symon going into the safe to hand me out the money. It's daft when you think of the money nowadays. But as a plumber I was earning £7. 10 shillings a week. At Ibrox I was offered £16 a week. More than double your money. It seemed a lot then. But when I think back I have to smile when I realise that the highest I was ever paid at Ibrox was £45 a week basic. In fact, when I finished up in the game with Dundee United in the late '60s I was only getting £30 a week.'

Unfortunately for Millar, Rangers were not the only people who wanted him to sign on. The '50s were the days of National Service, and three games into his career as a Rangers player Jimmy found himself in the uniform of the Royal Scots Fusiliers. And the not-so-lucky Jim didn't get the kind of break of others who followed him. 'I wasn't give a cushy posting at Stirling or Edinburgh or anything like that to let me keep on playing for Rangers. The troubles were on in Cyprus, and that's where I was sent. It took two vital years out of my career.'

He did learn to box a bit, and became regimental middle-weight champion. But he wanted to be a footballer, not a fighter. 'I had got the taste of what it was like being a Rangers first-team man two weeks after I joined the club,' he says. 'I made my first-team debut against Dundee, wearing the No. 10 jersey and up against the formidable Tommy Gallacher.' It was a losing debut for Jimmy. Dundee won 2-1 with two early goals from Christie and Merchant before Billy Simpson pulled one back in the 50th minute.

That was on January 29, 1955. And the teams were:
Dundee: Brown; Gray, Craig; Gallacher, Malloy, Cowie; Chalmers, Henderson, Merchant, Roy, Christie.
Rangers: Niven; Little, Cox; McColl, Young, Prentice; Waddell, Paton, Simpson, Millar, Hubbard. 'I was a boy playing with legends,' says Jimmy.

He managed one more League game, a 1-1 draw against St. Mirren at Ibrox, and a Scottish Cup tie against Aberdeen at Pittodrie on February 19. Rangers lost that one 2-1, so their new recruit had to swop the Ibrox blue for the Army brown

Ready to pounce. Millar stands by for goalmouth action.

without ever getting the taste of victory . . . or laying his hands on a win bonus.

However, before he was shipped to Cyprus he did manage two more games in the Rangers colours. One of them was in the League Cup semi-final at Hampden against Aberdeen on October 1 . . . and again he was on the losing side as Dons edged through 2-1 with goals from Leggat and Wishart against one from Hubbard for Rangers. 'I was beginning to wonder if Rangers ever won a game!' said Millar, who almost scored his first goal for the club in that match which was watched by 80,000. But his fierce left-foot shot which looked a scorer all the way was diverted on to the post by Dons international keeper Freddie Martin.

This feeling was enhanced when a week later Private Millar took his leave of Rangers in a League game against Airdrie at Ibrox in a game where the home club scored four times . . . and still couldn't win! They were 2-0 down, then 3-1 down and then 4-1 down before scoring three times in the last 15 minutes. Stirring stuff, but it still meant Millar had not been able to take a victory salute.

One Charity Cup tie while home on leave was all he could manage in season 1956-57, a year when Rangers won the championship for the 30th time. 'I knew I was losing valuable time in my career, but there was nothing I could do about it,' says Jimmy.

He got the winning feeling for the first time on August 17th, 1957 when Rangers beat Raith Rovers 4-3 at Ibrox in a League Cup tie before a 47,000 crowd. He was still not an accepted first team regular, but soon became one. For that very same League Cup competition was to throw up the result that brought dramatic changes in the Ibrox line-up . . . Celtic 7, Rangers 1.

Millar had played in the 4-0 semi-final win over Brechin, but missed the Final. 'That was definitely a lucky break!' says Jimmy. The week after the Hampden débâcle, he was in at left-half alongside Willie Moles who was the replacement centre-half for the man who carried the can for the caning . . . Johnny Valentine.

The Millar man was on his way. He made his European debut in the second leg of the first-round tie against St. Etienne in France; and played in the next two rounds against A.C. Milan. But he had to wait a long time before he could savour

Together again. Millar and his old Ibrox partner Ralph Brand when they linked up with Raith Rovers after leaving Rangers.

the pleasure of scoring. That turned out to be in a Scottish Cup quarter-final against Queen of the South when he and Max Murray bagged a double each in the 4-3 win.

'Once I found the way to the net, there was no looking back,' jokes Jimmy. Four days after the Cup tie, he scored the winner two minutes from time in a 3-2 Ibrox win over Falkirk . . . his first League goal. Four more followed by the end of the season.

Yet, it was to be another year before Millar really made his mark. His appearances were limited to a mere 10 in 1958-59. But going into the '60s, Rangers were putting together the side that was to dominate Scottish football for the next few years. Ian McMillan had been bought in from Airdrie; Jim Baxter was to follow from Raith Rovers. And the most famous partnership of the time was formed . . . Millar and Brand.

'We were just right for each other,' says Jimmy. 'Ralphie was ahead of his time, you know. He was a nag. Always wanting to try out something new. He nipped my head every week with his ideas. We linked naturally, but we also worked at it. Put in extra time at training. My strength was winning the ball, holding it and releasing it through to Ralphie who could cover so much ground so quickly that he was almost unmarkable at times. His running off the ball was tremendous. And that's what I always feel separates good teams from the rest. The guy off the ball is the key man. He can make you look good if he does the right thing to help. Ralphie did that for me for years. Quite a few teams in the '60s suffered from a dose of the old M and B.'

The partnership was not in place when Millar topped the League goal charts at Ibrox in 1959-60 with 21 scored in 30 games. Plus another six in the Scottish Cup, five in the League Cup and two in Europe. Included was his first hat-trick, netted in a 6-0 League win over Clyde and the winner 30 seconds from time in the Ne'erday game against Celtic. And he also picked up the first of his five Scottish Cup medals . . . scoring both goals in the 2-0 Hampden victory over Kilmarnock. A crowd of 108,017 watched these teams in action:

Rangers: Niven; Caldow, Little; McColl, Paterson, Stevenson; Scott, McMillan, Millar, Brand, Wilson.

Kilmarnock: Brown; Richmond, Watson; Beattie, Toner, Kennedy; Stewart, McInally, Kerr, Black, Muir.

The season was also notable for the European run Rangers had that year . . . all the way to the semi-finals before running into a German blitzkrieg called Eintracht Frankfurt. 'They beat us 12-4 on aggregate,' says Jimmy. 'Then they were duffed 7-3 by Real Madrid in the Final at Hampden. Maybe it's a good job we never got through. Real might have taken 20 off us! We were awfully naive, tactically. Just played it off the cuff whereas the Continentals were so well drilled and prepared. The clash in styles did lead to some interesting confrontations, mind you, over the years.'

In that Euro-run in '59-60 Jimmy was ordered off in the away leg against Red Star of Belgrade. 'They had a very good

The Boy Millar . . . Jimmy in his early days at Ibrox before he was called up for National Service.

player called Tichy who just kept on kicking me until I could stand it no more. I banjoed him and was ordered off. I was never in awe of anyone. And nobody ever scared me.'

But there was a price to be paid for his courage and determination. The swinging '60s arrived at Ibrox along with the '60s swinger Jim Baxter. Vintage years for Rangers . . . and Jimmy Millar. But Millar paid in pain for the good life. 'I injured my back against St. Johnstone on January 14, 1960. It turned out to be a slipped disc. I wasn't even 26 at the time, but that injury was to stay with me all the way through my career.'

Millar spent two weeks on boards at Phillipshill Hospital, more time in traction with weights on his feet, and didn't kick a ball again competitively for five months . . . then made his comeback in a European Final! 'I was pitched straight back into the first team to try to save the tie against Fiorentina in the Cup Winners' Cup Final,' he recalls. 'We had lost 2-0 at home in the first leg, and it was always going to be a losing struggle in Italy for the second game, although we were drawing 1-1 at one point before a great wee Swedish player called Kurt Hamrin scored a magnificent second goal for the Italian side.'

Despite his late season troubles, Millar picked up the first of three League Cup medals when Rangers beat Kilmarnock 2-0 at Hampden on October 29 with goals from Brand and Scott.

The next three years were to be golden ones for Millar and Rangers. From 1961 to 1964 the side swept to triumph with two League titles; two League Cups; and three Scottish Cups. 'Just about unbeatable in Scotland' is Millar's verdict on that side. 'We had a tremendous mixture of skill, strength, cunning and goal-scorers.' All qualities which Millar himself possessed!

Brand, Millar and Wilson scored 90 goals between them in the three major home competitions in season 1961-62. They then proceeded to top that by scoring 105 the next season!

Millar and Brand scored two of the goals which defeated Hearts 3-1 in the 1961 League Cup Final replay at Hampden; Brand and Wilson got the two goals which won the Scottish Cup against St. Mirren. And the same pairing did the damage the following year to beat Celtic 3-0 in the Scottish Final replay at Hampden.

The Scottish Cup hat-trick was completed in the treble-chance season of 1963-64, and it was a dose of the old M and B which proved too much for Dundee to swallow. 'It was a tremendous Final,' recalls Millar. 'Bert Slater had a fantastic game in goal for Dundee and it wasn't until midway through

Against all odds . . . Millar battles for the ball with two Partick Thistle defenders. The goalkeeper is former Ibrox colleague George Niven.

the second half I managed to beat him with a header from a corner. But wee Kenny Cameron scored the best goal of the game a minute later and we seemed to be heading for a replay until I got another with a header a minute from time, then Ralphie poached another just on the final whistle.'

Rangers were never able to match that 'high' again and the great days of the '60s proceeded at a more sedate pace with the 1-0 Scottish Cup Final victory over Celtic in 1966 the only time Jimmy added to his medal collection.

At international level, Millar's qualities were never recognised as they should have been. He won only two caps . . . and never got through 90 minutes either time! 'My first cap was against Austria at Hampden — and the English referee Jim Finney abandoned the game after 79 minutes because it was

Jumping for joy. Luckily a young John Greig is strong enough to take the strain as Millar goes all aboard following Greig's hat-trick goal in a 1962 League Cup tie against St. Mirren.

sheer mayhem. We were leading 4-1 at the time, and the Austrians were down to nine men because they had one player ordered off and another stretchered off. Then another was sent packing and a mini-battle broke out. The referee decided in the interests of everyone's safety that he should call a halt to proceedings.

'I was capped again a month later against Eire in Dublin . . . but pulled a muscle and was replaced by Ian St. John.' Jimmy also won League caps against England, the Irish League, the League of Ireland and Italy.

His career at Ibrox petered out in the mid-60s, ending on a sour note when he became involved in a too-public confrontation with a group of fans. 'They were giving me a lot of stick. I wasn't playing well, but clearly a section of the fans thought I was deliberately not laying off the ball to one of the

That's another one. Millar pops one into the net against Partick Thistle . . . just one of the 160 goals he netted for Rangers.

new boys in the team, Jim Forrest. I lost the place, and gave them the old Queen Victoria salute. Not just once. But half a dozen times. It was daft, and I regret it now. But at the time I was so frustrated with myself I just couldn't help it.'

Jimmy left Ibrox on a free transfer on June 11, 1967, having scored 160 goals in 317 matches. A month later he signed for Dundee United, linking up with his brother Tommy and earning a 'princely' £30 a week. By then he had established himself in his pub, sinking his lifetime earnings of £2,500 into the venture, and borrowing the rest. 'I was just 29 when I took over the pub. I was looking to the future and didn't fancy going back to being a plumber. It's very much a one-man business, but that's how I like it.'

What he doesn't like is the modern game with its 'too defensive tactics' and play-acting. 'I can't stand those guys who fall down and roll over at any excuse. I can't ever recall getting a penalty I didn't deserve. If I went down it was because I was hit. If I stayed down it was because I was hurt.'

Jimmy stayed with Dundee United for a couple of seasons, and enjoyed played alongside his brother. 'Tommy hated the Old Firm, you know. When we played Rangers for the first time, he was in the dressing room shouting "Come on lads, let's get into these Orange bastards". I just looked at him, and burst out laughing. But when it came to Celtic he was up there shouting: "Let's get into these Fenians". There was no discrimination. He disliked the two of them.'

There was also a short spell as manager of Raith Rovers, when he signed Ralph Brand to play for him. 'Almost got Jim Baxter, too, when he left Nottingham. But Rangers made him a better offer. I didn't really take to management. I don't think I had the ability to spot a player and then mould him.'

Nowadays Jimmy, a grandfather, relaxes with a game of golf when he can. And he's proud of the fact that one of his sons, Jim, is an international bowler and another boy, David, is a one-handicap golfer.

And he enjoys telling the Hearts fans who come into the pub about what he regards as one of his best games for Rangers . . . at right back! 'We lost goalkeeper Billy Ritchie after only eight minutes. Bobby Shearer had to go in goal and I moved to right-back. We beat Hearts 3-1 and I can't ever remember enjoying myself as much.'

Jimmy Millar's honours:

1963

May	Austria	(h)	4-1
	(Abandoned, 79 mins)		
June	Republic of Ireland	(a)	0-1

Millar also won League International Honours in 1962 against the Irish League, The English League and the Italian League. He was also capped against the League of Ireland in 1965.

CHAPTER 5

Davie Wilson

DAVIE WILSON IS A FOOTBALL JUNKIE. FROM the first days in the Lanarkshire village of Cambuslang when his miner father encouraged him to kick a ball, until now in his 50s, he has quite simply been hooked on the game.

He still plays five-a-side football twice a week and turns out in Old Crock games up and down the country most weekends. He is in love with the game, and openly admits it. 'In fact, when I was boss for a spell at Queen of the South I turned out in a reserve game because we were short of players. And I was 50 at that point,' he recalls. The fact that he can do all this is testimony to a lifetime of non-smoking, non-drinking and simply staying fit.

The wee fair-haired businessman in the pinstriped suit (which goes naturally with his role as a financial adviser in his own Carrington P.F.A. company) might just be the fittest company director in the country. But I doubt if any other City business type shares the same hobby as Davie . . . or rises before 5 a.m. every morning to indulge it.

Davie learned a love of pigeons from his father, and out in Cambuslang he maintains one of the biggest racing lofts in the country. 'I'm up every morning before five and over at the loft to see the birds,' says Davie. 'I have had a few successes in big races,' he says. 'Even in my playing days I would be up early to set the birds off on race mornings on a Saturday.'

It's a passion he shares with another well-known footballing character, Partick Thistle boss John Lambie, and

49

the two are in touch at least a couple of times a week. 'There are some people who say we're doo-lally,' jokes Davie.

It was his father Tom who encouraged Davie all the way through his footballing career . . . even though at first it was costing him a fortune. 'When I was a youngster at Gateside School, my old man promised me a shilling for every goal I scored. I was getting two or three at a time, so I don't know how he did it on a miner's wages. Eventually he had to give up.'

By that time Wilson junior was on his way to stardom with club and country. His prolific scoring had prompted scout Jocky Howison to take the wee Cambuslang schoolboy over to Ibrox for a training session at the age of 13. He was farmed out to Baillieston Juniors, who were then coached by former Ibrox captain Jock Shaw.

'My biggest disappointment at that time was that Cambuslang Rangers, my local team, wouldn't take me. They said I was too wee. So it gave me a lot of pleasure when I scored with a header in my first game against them.' Junior football taught Davie a lot: 'For a start, I learned that if you beat a man once, that was enough,' he says.

Wilson was 17 when he was called up to Ibrox as a player. And he found himself in a reserve team which contained Ralph Brand, Harry Melrose, Jimmy Millar, Harold Davis and Billy Ritchie. 'There were a few future internationalists in that lot,' he observes.

Including, of course, Davie Wilson who went on to win 22 full Scotland honours. But there was a learning process to go through at Ibrox before that happened. 'I had to do all the traditional jobs — clean the dressing rooms, look after the boots. And it had to be done right.' Particularly to suit the legendary names who were still first-team regulars when the boy Wilson was brushing out the dressing rooms.

'The likes of big George Young kept the youngsters in line,' says Davie. 'In fact I remember when I was going out for my debut match in the first team against Dundee at Dens Park,

Who's a happy boy then? Davie Wilson leaps high in the air as Jimmy Millar rushes to congratulate him after scoring the second goal in the 2-0 Scottish Cup Final win over St. Mirren in 1962.

I got a boot up the backside from big Corkie, who told me there was dust on his boots and it had better not happen again!'

Wilson got his first taste of the big time on January 2, 1957 against Partick Thistle at Ibrox. Still a teenager and still with that zest for goals which was to bring him 165 in the 11 seasons he was an Ibrox regular. There was no goal that debut day, but a victory at least in a 3-2 success for a Rangers team which read: Niven; Shearer, Caldow; McColl, Young, Davis; Scott, Simpson, Murray, Baird and Wilson.

There was no automatic place for the young Wilson, however, and he made only half a dozen other appearances in the rest of that season. But he did get the first of his many goals for Rangers . . . the last one in a 5-2 victory over Motherwell at Fir Park.

However, like most young men in those days, Davie found his services required elsewhere. By the Royal Engineers, in fact, and he spent two years of his National Service at Aldershot. 'I wouldn't say I did a lot of soldiering,' says Davie. 'Apart from getting a lot of time off to play for Rangers, I was playing for the British Army team nearly every week. We had some side. It included Alex Parker and Bert Slater of Falkirk, big Tubby Ogston of Aberdeen, Jackie Plenderleith of Hibs, Johnny Lawlor, John White and English fellows like Gerry Hitchens and Peter Dobbin. You could nearly have won the League with that side.'

Being a conscript limited Davie's outings for a couple of seasons. He played only a dozen League games in '57-58, scoring a couple more goals.

But he did get his first taste of European football . . . and, naturally, he scored! That was against St. Etienne, the French champions, in the return away leg on September 25, 1957 when Davie came into the team for flu-victim Johnny Hubbard and netted the only goal as Rangers went down 2-1 . . . but qualified for the next round on a 4-3 aggregate.

Alex Scott and Andy Matthew, signed from East Fife for £4,500 were the Rangers first-choice wingers in '58-59, but despite this and National Service, Davie managed 15 League appearances and half-a-dozen League Cup games in that season. He also won his first international recognition . . . capped at Under-23 level against Wales at Tynecastle when the Scots went down 1-0.

Wilson was on the verge of really crashing the big-time: and inside the next four seasons he crammed in the lot . . . caps, cup medals and fame. 'But the greatest pleasure of all was not the medals or honours . . . it was seeing the look of sheer pride in my father's face after every game,' says Davie. 'I was repaying all those bobs he forked out for my schoolboy goals. He was loving it, and so was I.'

So were the Rangers supporters as under Scot Symon the club struck a rich vein of success. League champions in 1961,

Victory salute. Davie Wilson, Eric Caldow and Billy Ritchie take the 1962
Scottish Cup on a trip round Hampden.

'63 and '64; Scottish Cup winners in '60, '62, '63 and '64; and
League Cup holders in '61, '62, '64 and '65. 'God, that team
was almost unbeatable at times,' recalls Davie.

'Jimmy Millar, Ralph Brand and myself would be striking
up bets on who would score the first goal in every game. And
we were getting plenty. You know, Jim Baxter might have been
the public star of stars in that team, but Jimmy Millar was a far
better player for the side. Even when he was injured, or didn't
feel like playing, he would still produce it. He was strong, he
was quick over the first few yards, he had control and he was
good in the air. He was also pretty crabbit at times, but the next
day after bawling you out he would come and sit beside you for
a talk.'

Wilson's contribution to the golden years was considerable. Early on he developed the knack of being in the right

place at the right time. 'Usually the back post,' he says. 'I'm still surprised at the number of players who don't make a bee-line for the back post when play is sweeping down the other side. I got a lot of goals simply because the ball would come shooting across the line of the defence leaving me with a clear chance.'

But there was a lot more to Wilson than that. He had gone off to the army a brown-haired boy and came back a beach blond. 'Bleached by the sun,' he would insist. In Aldershot? Whatever the cause, the Wilson mop was eye-catching in the Denis Law mould. So was his quick mind which compensated for the lack of devastating wing speed. So was his two-footed control and his willingness to play anywhere for the team. 'It didn't all just happen,' says Davie. 'There was a lot of natural talent in our team, but Millar, Brand and myself would be back in the afternoons a couple of days a week to work on moves and tactics. The trainer Davie Kinnear would chase us off the pitch at times.

'Fifteen years after I stopped playing with Rangers I was in an Old Crocks match alongside Ralphie Brand and I shouted one of the old signals to him . . . and he reacted straight away, and I scored. It was ingrained in us, I guess. Looking back, I believe that if we had been working with a really good coach, we had the team to win the European Cup. Scot Symon was a very fine man and a good motivator. But he never put on a tracksuit and worked with us. If we had been under someone like Jock Stein, we would have been European champions.'

The European dream may have eluded Rangers; little else did. From season 1959-60 when he made the breakthrough permanently, there was never a season when Davie Wilson was not adding to his collection. He got his first Scottish Cup badge at Hampden on April 23, when a Jimmy Millar double saw off Kilmarnock before a crowd of 108,017. Davie had scored seven goals in the Cup run (more than Millar) and finished the season with 23 competitive goals.

By the next season, Rangers had been Baxter-ised . . . and

In for the kill. Davie skips beyond Dundee defenders Ian Ure and Alex Hamilton to move in on a pass from the watching Jim Baxter.

the £17,500 signing of Slim Jim from Raith Rovers put the final touches to Scot Symon's dream team. Rangers all but swept the boards that first year AB (after Baxter). They won the title by a point from Kilmarnock, scoring 88 goals (Third Lanark netted 100 and were third!). Kilmarnock were the unfortunate victims again at Hampden as Rangers took the League Cup 2-0. They also reached the final of the Cup Winners Cup, but lost out to Fiorentiana of Italy over two legs and were stunned by a 5-2 replay thrashing from Motherwell in the third round of the Scottish Cup. Davie's contribution to all this came in the shape of 23 goals, 19 of them in the League. He played in every competitive game in that season.

The next year brought another Cup double and 28 goals from Wilson . . . six of them scored in one unforgettable game at Brockville when he was drafted in at centre-forward to replace the injured Jimmy Millar. Falkirk must have thought they were getting a lucky break, since Millar had scored a hat-trick against them in the earlier game at Ibrox. But the deputy centre turned out to be twice as troublesome. 'The ball just kept on hitting the net,' chuckles Davie. But I doubt if Falkirk

keeper Willie Whigham was laughing as he fetched the ball out
seven times in all. For the record, Davie's goals came in 24, 47,
52, 55, 63 and 82 minutes. That was on March 17. Four days
later Davie rattled in a hat-trick as the Scottish League beat
their heavily fancied English counterparts at Aston Villa's
ground.

'But I didn't get to wear the No. 9 jersey for long. Rangers
had a better man for the job in Jimmy Millar, and I didn't
mind giving it up,' says Davie. He was in the team that beat
Hearts 3-1 in the League Cup Final replay and scored his first
Hampden final goal in the 2-0 Scottish Cup success against St
Mirren on April 21.

Rangers kept things going at the double once again in
'62-63, and it was evident that the coveted grand slam of all
three major Scottish trophies was a possibility. Rangers
notched up 94 League goals from 34 games: Davie Wilson hit
23 of them, and added 10 more in other matches for a total of
33.

'And I still trailed Jimmy Millar by 10 and Ralph Brand by
seven!' says Davie. 'That's how hot we were.'

But it wasn't just for his club that Wilson was making his
mark. He had won his first full cap against Wales at Cardiff on
October 22, 1960, and although the Scots lost 2-0, he was in
again for the meeting with Northern Ireland at Hampden in
November which was won 5-2. Even the catastrophe of the 9-3
defeat by England at Wembley — Davie scored his first goal
for Scotland that day — didn't stop his cap climb. He played
13 times out of Scotland's next 16 games, scoring five times. In
all, Davie netted nine times in his 22 games. None gave him
more pleasure than the opener in the 2-0 victory over England
at Hampden in 1962.

He didn't score in the next meeting with England at
Wembley . . . but played a key role in the 2-1 victory. 'When
Eric Caldow went down early on following a tackle from big
Bobby Smith, we all heard the crack, and knew what had
happened. Eric was stretchered off with a broken leg . . . and I

Country Boy. Davie is a lover of the great outdoors . . . with fishing as one of his hobbies.

was drafted in at left-back by team boss Ian McColl. I would have played anywere for Scotland, and the fact that we won with 10 men was all the better.'

Medals by the handful. Davie shows off some of his Ibrox collection. He won a grand total of nine League, Scottish and League Cup honours.

'Handy' is hardly the word to describe Davie. He reckons he played in every position in senior football except centre-half. 'That I WAS too wee for,' he says. 'But I would have done it if asked.' Since he played with distinction in goal a couple of times — once stepping in at Pittodrie after Norrie Martin fractured his skull against Aberdeen — he no doubt would have done the job well.

Inevitably, English clubs often wanted Wilson to come down their way. 'In fact I could have been Britain's first £100,000 player' he recalls. 'Everton were prepared to pay Rangers £99,999 for me in 1961, but Scot Symon blocked the move. I would probably have gone, since I was getting £40 a week at Ibrox and Everton were offering £100.'

He stayed, but unfortunately a broken ankle received in the League Cup semi-final victory over Berwick Rangers on

City Slicker. The former Rangers winger, who is now a financial consultant in Glasgow, is clearly dressed for business.

October 2, 1963 put him out of action for several months during that great Rangers side's most successful season of al . . . the treble-winning team of 1963-64.

He didn't play again until February, and thus managed only 16 League games in that season. Yet he still managed six League goals, six more in the League Cup and four in the Scottish Cup, where he won the fourth of his five medals when Rangers beat Dundee 3-1.

Davie's last major honour won with Rangers was in the 1966 Scottish Cup final replay against Celtic . . . the night Celts were sent Kai-high as the Ibrox Danish right-back Kai Johansen rammed in a 25-yarder for the only goal of the game in the 70th minute.

The old guard were being marched out: Brand had already gone to Manchester City; Jimmy Millar was given a free and signed for Dundee United in July, only to be re-united with Wilson a month later in a swop deal which saw flying Swede Orjan Persson move to Ibrox.

Davie played nearly 400 top competitive games for Rangers, and scored 165 goals. Not bad going for someone rated too wee by his local team.

He played on at Tannadice for another five seasons, and moved to Dumbarton for two more seasons before becoming manager. He was with Queen of the South and Kilmarnock in managerial posts but now confines himself to 'a wee bit of scouting'.

He enjoys watching the new Rangers, but believes Graeme Souness gave up being a player far too soon. 'He is the best thing in Scottish football in 30 years. To me he was Jim Baxter, but harder. He had the talent but not the cheek of Slim Jim, but was far more aggressive. He had a lot more to give as a player.'

It wouldn't be right to finish the Wilson story without reference to his well-known ability as one of football's great 'divers' in the '60s. 'He could be fouled in the centre-spot and nearly get a penalty' one defender observed to me at the time. How was it done? 'I told you earlier. Hard work, and even harder practice,' says Davie with just the hint of a smile.

Davie Wilson's honours:

1960

Oct.	Wales	(a)	0-2
Nov.	Northern Ireland	(h)	5-2

1961

Apr.	England	(a)	3-9
May	Republic of Ireland	(h)	4-1
May	Republic of Ireland	(a)	3-0
May	Czechoslovakia	(a)	0-4
Sept.	Czechoslovakia	(h)	3-2
Oct.	Northern Ireland	(a)	6-1
Nov	Czechoslovakia	(n)	2-4
	(Play-off, Belgium)		(aet)

1962

Apr.	England	(h)	2-0
May	Uruguay	(h)	2-3
Oct.	Wales	(a)	3-2

1963

Apr.	England	(a)	2-1
May	Austria	(h)	4-1
	(Abandoned after 79 mins)		
June	Norway	(a)	3-4
June	Republic of Ireland	(a)	0-1
June	Spain	(a)	6-2

1964

Apr.	England	(h)	1-0
May	West Germany	(a)	2-2
Nov.	Northern Ireland	(a)	3-2

1965

Apr.	England	(a)	2-2
May	Finland	(a)	2-1

CHAPTER 6

Ron McKinnon

AMONG THE MEDALS AND TROPHIES ON SHOW in Mrs Anne McKinnon's display cabinet in her home in Glasgow's Mosspark area, there is a strange-looking metal plate with a dozen screws. Not the normal football memento you would find among a proud mother's collection. But it is there because of the significance it had in the life of her son, Rangers and Scotland centre-half Ronnie McKinnon.

That now useless piece of metal once held Ronnie's broken leg together. But it couldn't hold his career together, and at his peak and with a few good years at the top still ahead of him, Ronnie bowed out of top-class football. 'One tackle, one shattering moment turned my life upside down,' says the still-slim six-footer who left Scotland 17 years ago and is now in residence in South Africa.

'I felt I was in my prime, already capped 28 times for Scotland and with a collection of League and Cup medals. All I wanted now was to add a European trophy to complete the set. And the way we were playing in 1971-72, we all considered that at long last Rangers were about to break their duck in Europe.'

They did, going on to win the Cup Winners' Cup Final in the game in Barcelona that is unfortunately better remembered for the after-match battle between the fans and the police than the 3-2 victory over Moscow Dynamo.

But McKinnon was only a spectator that wild Spanish summer night on May 24, 1972 . . . confined to a seat in the stand by a tackle in another Latin city six months earlier. That

Dressed to impress. Ronnie McKinnon is dapperly turned out as he heads for a meeting with the S.F.A. Referee Committee at the Association Headquarters in Park Gardens, Glasgow.

tackle — an accidental one, Ronnie stresses — came halfway through one of the most dramatic games in Rangers' long European history. Rangers were in Lisbon on the return leg of a second-round tie against Sporting. 'We had beaten them 3-2 at Ibrox, but despite having lost those two goals at home were still confident of going through simply because we felt we would score a few goals ourselves in the away game.' says Ronnie. This confidence was justified. For although Yazalde netted in the 26th minute to tie the aggregate, Colin Stein netted a minute later. He did the same early in the second half after Tome had scored in the 37th minute.

But halfway through the second half came the moment that all footballers dread. 'I went into what looked like a normal tackle . . . fell awkwardly with my opponent and there was a crack that was heard all over the ground. Everyone knew right away it was a break. So did I, of course, and I think I was sitting up signalling for a stretcher even before our physio Tom Craig made it on the pitch.'

That was the beginning of a nightmare couple of days for McKinnon, the quiet man of the Ibrox dressing room. As his team-mates carried on the battle, with Dave Smith brought on to operate in defence in place of his injured colleague, Ronnie was on his way to a Lisbon hospital. 'I spent the whole night in a hospital ward with people dying all around me. The leg was so badly broken that the local surgeon did not feel qualified to touch it and said it would need a specialist to do the job.'

That specialist was back in Glasgow at the Victoria Infirmary, and getting to him is a trip Ronnie will never forget. 'Mind you I can safely say at the time it was all happening in a dream-like way,' he says. 'I was so drugged up with morphine I was high long before I was flying!'

Rangers took out a row of seats in their chartered KLM flight back to Glasgow and McKinnon returned home with the team only vaguely aware that he was travelling with a party who weren't sure whether they were still in the Cup Winners' Cup. While McKinnon was on his way to hospital, Sporting had scored a late goal against the re-organised defence to take the game into extra time. Then in the extended period, first of all Henderson netted for Rangers and then Sporting equalised.

Mistakenly the Austrian referee ordered a penalty shoot-out, which Rangers lost. But one of the Scottish football

Action Man. McKinnon worked hard to overcome his early weakness in the air.

writers on the trip, the late John Mackenzie of the *Daily Express*, pointed out to Ibrox boss Willie Waddell that under the rules, Rangers had won the tie on away goals WHICH STILL COUNTED IN EXTRA TIME. But it was the next day before U.E.F.A. headquarters in Switzerland confirmed the fact. 'Meanwhile, I was totally oblivious to all the drama,' recalls Ronnie. 'I was still in orbit. Then when we got back to Glasgow and I was rushed to the Victoria, the surgeon Mr McDougall took one look and declared I would have to wait another day. He had been in the operating theatre all day and had eyes like a panda, he said. So it was six o'clock the following morning before he operated. And put in that metal plate and 12 screws which my mother keeps in the display cabinet at home.'

Eighteen months later and Ronnie's career with Rangers was over. He made only a few reserve appearances late in season 1972-73, and on April 27, 1973 he was freed from Ibrox and within weeks he was on his way to South Africa to play. And that is where he remains to this day.

McKinnon was born in Govan — he says that gives the lie to Alex Ferguson's claim to being the only good footballer ever born in that part of Glasgow — the elder of twin boys by two hours. 'I think it came as a bit of a shock to my parents, who didn't know until the last minute that twins were on the way,' says Ronnie. The family were teuchters — dad Murdo was from Skye and mother Anne from Stornoway. So the Gaelic language was a feature of the household.

The McKinnon twins both went into football, with Donnie playing at centre-half for Partick Thistle for many years before becoming the club's physio for a long spell.

Getting to the top was a long, hard road for Ronnie. He was only 16 when he signed for local Govan junior team Benburb. He was still 16 when the Bens had one of those shake-ups which are part of junior football, and a disappointed McKinnon found himself back in juvenile football. 'I didn't think I was going to make it at all at that point,' says Ronnie. But then Stirlingshire junior club Dunipace came on the scene. 'I was an inside-forward in those days, but then one day when we were due to meet Renfrew Juniors it was decided I would move back to left half to face their top player, a lad called Billy Young. I played well, and that was it. Half-back it was from then on.'

There was a signing offer from Clyde before Rangers came in for him, clearly upset at the idea of a boy from Govan going to play his football anywhere but Ibrox. 'They could easily have changed their minds after my first reserve game against

Footballing family. The young Ronnie McKinnon is pictured in his youthful days at home with father Murdo, mother Anne, brother Donnie and sister Anne.

Hibs,' recalls Ronnie. 'They tried me out at inside-forward again . . . and we lost 7-0. Some start! But by the next week I was back at wing-half and stayed in the reserve team for the whole of that '59-60 season.'

Ronnie made his first-team debut on March 8, 1961 in a 3-0 victory over Hearts at Ibrox, deputising for injured iron man Harry Davis at right half. Rangers had just added the

legendary Slim Jim Baxter to the staff, and another young man
who was making the breakthrough in that season from the
reserves was wee Willie Henderson. He was not in that debut
game for McKinnon. The teams that day were:
Rangers: Niven; Shearer, Caldow; McKinnon, Baillie,
Stevenson; Scott, McMillan, McLean, Brand, Wilson.
Hearts: Marshall; Kirk, Holt; Bowman, Milne, Cumming;
Smith, Murray, Davidson, Blackwood, Crawford.

Four days later, in a 2-1 win over Clyde, Henderson was in
the team for his debut.

But it was to be the next season before both McKinnon
and Henderson made a real first-team impact. And so did
another young man from the reserves . . . John Greig.

Ronnie had played in only one League game that season —
against Falkirk in a 4-0 win at Ibrox on November 18 — so by
the time the semi-final of the Scottish Cup came along in
March, 1962 he was still a rookie.

But the army changed all that. Not that he was
conscripted. Jim Baxter had been, though, and as Rangers
were taking the field against Motherwell at Hampden on
March 31, Private Baxter of the Black Watch was doing his
duty against the Belgian Army!

McKinnon was drafted in at left-half against 'Well, and
Rangers duly won 3-1. 'I guess I must have impressed,' says
Ronnie. 'For when Baxter came back the next week, manager
Scot Symon dropped big Doug Baillie from centre-half and
pushed me into that position for the first time.' Which must be
the first time anyone managed to push aside Baillie, a fearsome
6ft 2in, 15-stone figure.

Baillie and Bill Paterson had been sharing the No. 5 spot
most of the season, but manager Scot Symon was looking to
the future. And the future was McKinnon. Ronnie was in at
centre-half against St. Johnstone in a 4-0 away League win the
following week. And that was him from then on. His season
finished in style, too, with a Scottish Cup medal after playing
in just two ties!

Pace was McKinnon's greatest asset . . . as he shows here.

Rangers beat St. Mirren 2-0 in the Final at Hampden on April 21, 1962 with two goals from Ralph Brand in the 40th minute and Davie Wilson in the 57th. A crowd of 126,930 watched the game. The teams were:

Rangers: Ritchie; Shearer, Caldwell; Davis, McKinnon, Baxter; Henderson, McMillan, Millar, Brand, Wilson.

St. Mirren: Williamson; Campbell, Wilson; Stewart, Clunie, McLean; Henderson, Bryceland, Kerrigan, Fernie, Beck.

Ronnie McKinnon had arrived. But he was still learning.

'And I had to learn the hard way,' says Ronnie. 'I was very fast, and that was my main asset. But I wasn't convincing enough in the air.' This was never more evident than against Tottenham Hotspur in the Cup Winners' Cup ties near the end of 1962. Rangers were thrashed 5-2 at White Hart Lane and 3-1 at Ibrox. 'I took a lot of stick for my weakness in the air,' says Ronnie. 'Deservedly so. But I was just a boy in those games and I was looking for help but never found it. Everyone else was struggling as well. Of course, Spurs were a superb side. That was the days of Danny Blanchflower, Dave Mackay, John White, Bobby Smith and Jimmy Greaves. They were some side.'

It was clear the young McKinnon had a lot of work to do. And he did it. 'I went out to the training ground and spent hours heading away cross balls. It has still affected my head to this day.'

Despite the trauma of the Spurs games, young McKinnon still finished up with his first League medal as Rangers romped to the title, nine points clear of second-placed Kilmarnock. And there was a second successive Scottish Cup medal, won with a 3-0 Hampden replay victory over Celtic. A crowd of 129,527 watched the teams draw 1-1 in the first game, with the goals coming from Ralph Brand and then Bobby Murdoch within two minutes.

But in the replay, which was watched by 120,263, Rangers brought back veteran Ian McMillan and his genius at inside-forward set up a 3-0 victory with Brand scoring twice and Davie Wilson getting the other.

If the young McKinnon thought that was good . . . even better was to follow. Rangers completely dominated Scottish football, sweeping all before them as they romped to the title six points ahead of Kilmarnock; and thumped Morton 5-0 in the League Cup Final at Hampden (with Jim Forrest scoring

Talking it over. McKinnon and another favourite from the 60s and 70s . . . Willie Johnston.

four and his cousin Alex Willoughby getting the other). The Scottish Cup was won for the third year running. But it took Rangers a long time to overcome the defiance of Dundee goalkeeper Bert Slater. Indeed, it was only in the last 19 minutes that the deadly partnership of Brand and Millar found they way past him . . . both netting inside the last two minutes in a 3-1 win.

At the age of 23, Ronnie McKinnon was the possessor of a chestful of medals. Speed on the ground was his natural asset. But hard work had improved his capability to handle aerial combat.

He did have one tendency that startled his opponents and

distracted his team-mates . . . he liked to whistle while he worked! 'I think it unnerved the likes of Bobby Shearer and Davie Provan more than it did the opposition,' says Ronnie. 'But it was just a way of relaxing tension. Besides which, I WAS happy in my work.'

Which is a good job. For over the next few years a lot of hard work was to fall on the shoulders of McKinnon and his fiercely competitive companion John Greig. For the great Baxter-inspired era came to an end. Grind replaced the glory. Within a short space of time Baxter, Brand and Shearer were gone. The year after the treble was won the trophy room had a bare look. Only the League Cup was retained by virtue of a 2-1 win over Celtic.

But for McKinnon, that season did bring another memorable event . . . his first goal for the team. And spectacular it was. Rangers had gone to Belgrade, holding a 3-1 lead over Red Star in the first round of the European Cup. By the 77th minute the Slavs had swept into a 4-1 lead and the Ibrox club were heading for the door marked exit. 'I think there was less than a minute to go when I came up for a corner . . . and couldn't believe it when a Jim Forrest header thumped off the cross bar and came right to me. I headed it home. You would have thought we had won the Cup the way I carried on!'

McKinnon played in all 55 games for Rangers that season, and was a key figure. But there was no sign of the international cap that many people felt he was due. 'The trouble was, Scotland already had a fine centre half in Billy McNeill,' says Ronnie. 'He was a commanding figure, and was rightly considered the number one.'

Ironically, it was CELTIC manager Jock Stein who finally presented Ronnie with his first national honour. And what a game to make your debut: a life-or-death World Cup tie against the brilliant Italians before 100,000 screaming fans at Hampden.

McKinnon had been called into the pool for the game on November 9, 1965. 'But I wasn't expecting to play. So when

Standing by. McKinnon (left) watches the action as colleagues Sandy Jardine and Kai Johansen leap to clear the danger from Aberdeen's Jim Storrie during a 1967 League Cup tie at Ibrox.

Jock Stein rattled off the team at our headquarters in Largs, I wasn't really listening. I heard my name mentioned, but assumed I was being listed with the substitutes. But as we were all leaving, Stein called me back and told me I was in the team. He told me he was worried about the speed of the Italian centre-forward Mazzola, who was jet-propelled. He told me I had the speed to match him and I was in the team. I had tremendous respect for Stein after that. He was Celtic manager, but he made his choice on tactical grounds alone. He was a big man in every way.'

Scotland won that memorable game with a John Greig goal. But the World Cup dream ended two games later when a makeshift Scottish side crashed 3-0 to the Italians in Naples. By then McKinnon had a hold of the No. 5 jersey and was

73

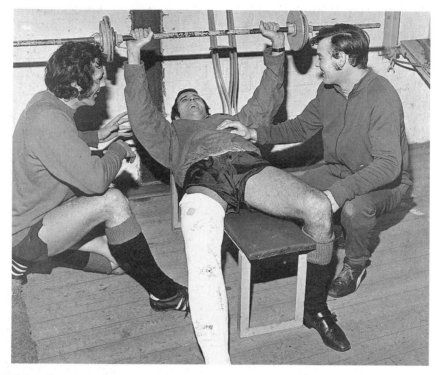

With a little help from his friends . . . Ronnie in the recovery room at Ibrox after his broken leg putting his shoulder into some weight training. With suitable encouragement from big Colin Jackson and physio Tommy Craig.

reluctant to let go. He missed only two of the next 19 internationals, and scored the winner in the 3-2 Hampden win over Wales on November 22, 1967.

In the present-day climate there would have been no problem of fielding both McKinnon and McNeill. But back in those days a central defender was a railway policeman in Glasgow's main station! Yet, the idea was experimented with twice: against England in a 1-1 draw at Hampden in 1968 and a 3-2 defeat at the hands of Germany in Hamburg on October 22, 1969. 'The way football is played nowadays, I think big Billy and myself could have formed a good partnership,' says Ronnie.

While McKinnon's international career prospered, his club days became a struggle. Celtic became almost invincible under the influence of Stein. When Danish full-back Kai Johansen hammered in a 70th-minute winner in the 1966

Howzat. The gear is a bit unfamiliar . . . the style looks good . . . but the ball is definitely not regulation size. McKinnon warms up in a charity cricket match watched by team-mate Dave Smith..

Scottish Cup Final replay against Celtic, no one knew that it was the last time Rangers were to strike silver for a long time. And when they did, five seasons later, it was McKinnon, captain in place of the injured Greig, who had the task of waving the League Cup aloft after a teenager called Derek

All ears and teeth . . . that's Ibrox duo John Greig and Ronnie McKinnon snapped doing some shopping on a trip abroad.

Johnstone had leaped high above Billy McNeill to head the ball past Evan Williams to give Rangers a 1-0 victory at Hampden on October 24, 1970.

The years between trophies might have been barren: but they were not uneventful. Scot Symon was sacked on November 1, 1967 with his team at the top of the table, but Celtic in South America competing for the World Club title. His assistant Davie White was promoted . . . only to suffer the same fate two years later. 'Symon was a man's man. He gave me my break and stood by me when I was being criticised. I will always be indebted to him for that. Davie White just didn't get time to learn the job.'

Whistle while you work . . . that was the McKinnon motto. A trait that irritated his team-mates and startled the opposition.

It was the fearsome Waddell-Wallace combination that put Rangers back on the trophy trail again. But sadly, McKinnon got very little time to enjoy the benefits accrued under that partnership. 'However, I have no complaints. I had great years at Ibrox. Played in great teams with great players.

'Jim Baxter was king, of course. On the field he was brilliant: off it, not so good. But he exuded such confidence that everyone was touched by it. He could thread a pass through the eye of a needle. But he was so arrogant. I can recall him in one game being the subject of some heavy treatment by a young player. Jim then proceeded to make the lad look foolish umpteen times, and said to him: "I hope you have a trade to fall back on, son."

'Willie Henderson was brilliant too. When he came into the team Scot Symon told me not to try anything smart, just get the ball out to Willie. And that's just what I did.

'But the greatest player of all as far as I am concerned was Denis Law. He had everything. He had two feet, he could jump tremendous heights. He could tackle and he was afraid of nothing. I always counted it a privilege to have played in the same team as Denis.'

Despite his new life thousands of miles from Scotland — Ronnie has re-married and has a six-year-old daughter — he keeps up with events in Europe via the games from many countries which are put out on the television. 'And my mother sends me cuttings from the papers. 'I'm out of football altogether now,' says Ronnie, who had spells as player and coach in Durban. He now works in car sales and says he is still as lean and fit as ever.

'Still as good looking, too,' he jokes. 'But when I bite into a steak nowadays I tend to leave my teeth in it.' He didn't mention whether he still whistles while he works. I hope so. Some traditions should never fade.

Ronnie McKinnon's honours:

1965

Nov.	Italy	(h)	1-0
Nov.	Wales	(h)	4-1
Dec.	Italy	(a)	0-3

1966

Apr.	England	(h)	3-4
May	Holland	(h)	0-3
June	Brazil	(h)	1-1
Oct.	Wales	(a)	1-1
Nov.	Northern Ireland	(h)	2-1

1967

Apr.	England	(a)	3-2
Oct.	Northern Ireland	(a)	0-1
Nov.	Wales	(h)	3-2

1968

Feb.	England	(h)	1-1
May	Holland	(a)	0-0
Oct.	Denmark	(a)	1-0
Nov.	Austria	(h)	2-1
Dec.	Cyprus	(a)	5-0

1969

Apr.	West Germany	(h)	1-1
Sept.	Republic of Ireland	(a)	1-1
Oct.	West Germany	(a)	2-3
Nov.	Austria	(a)	0-2

1970

Apr.	Northern Ireland	(a)	1-0
Apr.	Wales	(h)	0-0
Apr.	England	(h)	0-0
Nov.	Denmark	(h)	1-0

1971

Feb.	Belgium	(a)	0-3
Apr.	Portugal	(a)	0-2
June	Denmark	(a)	0-1
June	Russia	(a)	0-1

CHAPTER 7

Tom Forsyth

TOP GOALKEEPERS TEND TO BE REMEMBERED for their great saves; strikers for their spectacular goals. But few defenders are ever remembered for just ONE tackle they make among thousands. In Tom Forsyth's case it's different. He's remembered for a tackle in a million. Or maybe 'revered' is a better word since the tackle in question stopped England scoring and meant a Hampden victory for Scotland over the Auld Enemy. Victory that was deemed necessary in 1976, for England were still laying patronage following their 5-1 slaughtering of the Scots at Wembley the year before.

Scotland needed a result. And they needed a hero. Tom Forsyth provided both that Saturday afternoon on May 15, 1976.

Scotland were leading 2-1 thanks to a first-half goal from Don Masson and a second-half shot from Kenny Dalglish which did much to prove that England goalkeepers are NOT invincible: it may not be nice to mock the afflicted, but many Scottish fans still recall with relish the sight of the ball squirming through the arms of a hapless Ray Clemence and into the net off the keeper's knees.

However, late in the second half there was a moment when the pleasure of victory was about to be snatched away from the Scots. Big Southampton striker Mick Channon, scorer of England's opening goal, was off like one of the racehorses he owned in pursuit of a through ball. But one stride away from hitting what looked like a certain equaliser, the ball was

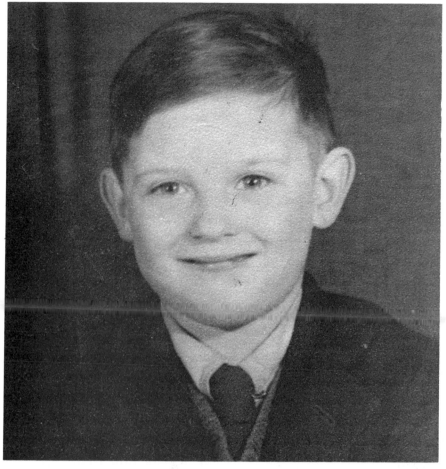

Tom Forsyth's school days.

wheeched away from his feet by a brilliantly timed Forsyth tackle.

'The ball had gone past me on my left side. I knew that I had to time my tackle just right, otherwise it was a penalty for sure,' recalls Tom. He did just that. And even to this day there are supporters who come up and shake his hand in heartfelt thanks.

Probably non-Rangers fans at that, who spent the rest of the time howling in anger as the big Ibrox defender dealt out a series of crunching takles on rivals up and down the country in a career which in 10 years brought him 23 caps, four Scottish Cup badges and two League and League Cup medals.

But glittering prizes were won at a price. Some forwards might have felt hard done by with the Forsyth robust style of play. 'But I think I did more damage to myself than any opponent,' says Tom, who is currently assistant manager to his old Ibrox colleague Tommy McLean at Motherwell.

Years of stretching sinews to the limit cost him dearly: two cartilage operations; a serious pelvic injury; and finally a major condition of the right knee which to this day still swells up like a balloon if he plays in a competitive practice game.

'It was the price I paid for my style of play,' says Tom. 'I will always deny that I was a dirty player. I went in hard, sure. But always for the ball. However, I admit the timing had to be right. Like the Channon tackle. Otherwise the effect looked really bad and led to a lot of bookings. But, of course, quite a few forwards played up to the situation and made a meal of any tackle. Play-acting is not a new complaint in football.'

One player who publicly lambasted Forsyth was Dundee United's Paul Sturrock, who described playing against Forsyth as being like 'facing a combine harvester'. He also admitted his deadliest rival was a good player 'but has a mean streak in him'. Forsyth dismisses any talk of a vendetta against the United man. 'Paul was a really good player. But he hated playing against me. I was no harder on him than I was on anyone else. He was frightened of playing aginst me, and that meant I won the psychological battle.'

Not every time. There was one occasion just before a Cup Final, when Forsyth was delicately placed on the bookings limit. One more offence would have put him out of the Final. 'Sturrock learned about this, and in the meeting with United just prior to the Final he tried to gain revenge for all the hard times I had given him, knowing full well I was tip-toeing on a tightrope. What he did was not entirely brave, but maybe it was understandable. He had to try to win one battle in his meetings with me.'

Forsyth's legendary tackling earned him the nickname of 'Jaws', a title he tried to pretend he didn't like at the time but

Lashing out with the left foot in training.

will now admit he actually quite enjoyed. 'It just meant I had to suffer a lot of ribbing from other players,' he says. 'But I never felt I was a dirty player. I was tough, but I tried to do the job I was picked for as honestly as I could. I liked to win, and that's how I played.'

Backing for Forsyth's view of his own ability has come over the years from colleagues like Colin Jackson, who played alongside Tom in the heart of the Ibrox defence: 'A fair tackler who goes in hard but is nowhere near a dirty player. He's too honest and straightforward for that. And the highly skilful

Bobby Graham of Motherwell, a player with a delicate touch on the ball, was moved to describe Forsyth as: 'hard, very hard. But not dirty. If he has a fault it is trying too hard to get to the ball, but I have never known him to stoop to underhand tactics.' This testimony also comes from a man who admits that on one occasion he tried to chat the big Rangers defender off his game . . . and paid for it. 'I warned him in advance that I was going to take him on down the wing and beat him. Sure enough I did. The next thing I knew he had caught up with me and the force of his tackle had me bouncing off the boundary wall!'

Balancing the praise, however, was the view back in 1975 from former Ibrox hard man Harry Davis: 'Forsyth is too hard. I never tried to intimidate players the way he does.'

All this hard-man talk seems strangely out of place when you meet Forsyth . . . tall, but not overly powerful, and with a very soft voice. And it seems even more incongruous when he talks of his hobbies . . . bowls, a bit of golf, and market gardening.

Tom was one of twin boys born in Paisley in 1949, and the Forsyth family moved to Stonehouse in Lanarkshire soon afterwards. Big Tom has remained there ever since. 'My twin Robert and I are like chalk and cheese. When we were kids at Stonehouse Primary HE was always bigger and stronger. I was a big skinny lump with hardly any strength.'

But by the time the twins reached their teens, and Tom was an appentice carpenter with George Wilson Joinery in Stonehouse, it was the younger of the two brothers — Tom by 25 minutes — who was beginning to make a mark in football. At the age of 16½ he was playing for the local junior club which, in the manner so beloved of so many small-town teams, was delicately addressed as 'The Violet'.

He was then signed as a professional player by then Motherwell manager Bobby Howitt, and turned professional once his time was out. 'I can't say I enjoyed full-time football at that point,' says Tom. 'There were only half a dozen of us.

All-round sportsman. Tom Forsyth shows two of the trophies he has won for his prowess on the bowling green.

And I would be back home at noon some days with nothing to do. I was used to working hard so it got to me for a while.'

But a breakthrough to first-team football in season 1967-68 changed all that. 'We were beaten 2-1 that first game by a Kilmarnock team which featured Billy Dickson, Kenny Cameron and two brothers called Jim and Tommy McLean.'

Years later Tom McLean and Tom Forsyth were to become an inseparable pairing at Ibrox: they travelled together to training every day in the same car and Forsyth was jokingly called wee Tam's minder . . . although a number of big defenders who took liberties with McLean were to discover that Forsyth took his 'Terry McCann' role seriously!

Tom played against Rangers at Ibrox on January 20, 1968 when the Light Blues won 2-0. And at the end of that season, Motherwell were relegated. They were back a year later, as Second Division champions. By this time Forsyth had drifted further back from his midfield role to play defensively alongside Willie McCallum, and a great career was beginning to take shape.

When Bobby Brown picked him for the Scotland Under-23 side against England at Hampden on February 24, 1971 it was clear the Forsyth saga had started. Scotland drew 2-2 that night and the team is worth considering: McRae; Jardine, Hay, Blackley, Connelly, Kelly, Young, Forsyth, Robb, Jarvie, Duncan.

Most went on to further fame and glory at club and full international level, Forsyth included. He played for the full squad for the first time against Denmark in a 1-0 defeat in Copenhagen on June 9, 1971. And also that year was in the Scottish League side which lost 1-0 at Hampden to England . . . a result repeated when Forsyth played in the very last of these games in 1976.

By then he was a Rangers player. Jock Wallace wanted him, and succeeded with a £45,000 offer on October 11, 1972. But Forsyth didn't even get to leave Fir Park to make his debut. Four days later he lined up against Motherwell in a 2-0 Rangers victory! The teams that day were:

Motherwell: MacRae, Whiteford, Wark; Watson, McCallum, Goodwin; Gray, Martin, McCabe, Lawson, Heron.

Rangers: McCloy, Jardine, Mathieson; Greig, Johnstone, Smith; Conn, Forsyth, Parlane, Mason, Young.

But there was to be a stuttering start to his Ibrox career for Forsyth. 'I struggled through the first three games and was getting a lot of stick. But if that wasn't bad enough, I then badly pulled a hamstring and was out of the team for the next two months,' recalls Tom. In fact it was two days before Christmas before he saw first-team action again, in a 4-0 victory over East Fife at Bayview.

The fans were still sceptical. But they changed their minds when the big fellow performed heroically in the 2-1 victory over Celtic at Ibrox on January 6, 1973. 'He has proved to me he has arrived,' commented boss Wallace. 'He never knows when he is beaten, wants to win everything and gives 100 per cent. And he wants to play football all the time.'

Star on the street. Forsyth mucks in with the schoolkids in his home town of Stonehouse in his days as a Motherwell player.

Any remaining sceptics were converted on May 5, 1973 when Forsyth stepped in with a footballing contribution that for some people carries even more significance than his tackle on Channon. Rangers beat Celtic in the Scottish Cup Final 3-2, to pick up the trophy for the first time since 1966. And the man who did the trick was none other than Forsyth, who scored one of the most celebrated Scottish Cup Final goals in modern times. Celebrated because not only was it his first for the club, and also the winner, but because he almost missed it from 12 inches! Big Derek Johnstone, whose header hit one post and rolled along the line to tap the other post, swears blind to this day that if Forsyth had been wearing short studs he would have missed!

Says Tom: 'Celtic had pulled a goal back through Kenny Dalglish a few minutes earlier to tie the score at 2-2. When we got a free kick in the 60th minute, I decided for once to desert the sweeper's role and get up into the box. I was following up when Johnstone headed in and couldn't believe it when the ball bounced off the second post and landed at my feet. I got a helluva fright. I had gone too far and was ahead of it and nearly missed. It would have been hard for me to do but I almost did.' He didn't, and the Cup went to Ibrox. But to this day, that goal causes hilarity in the Forsyth household. 'A supporters' club gave me a video of it. I had never really studied it closely till then. But my son David loves to run it. He's in knots every time he sees it.'

Comical or not, that was the beginning of a glorious spell of success for Forsyth and Rangers. But not straight away. Celtic were having one last, final throw at the championship, winning it for the ninth successive season in 1973-74.

And Jock Wallace was still moulding together the team that was first of all to end Celtic's championship sequence in 1974-75, then go on a year later to corner the market in Scottish silverware. 'Jock is an amazing man,' says Forsyth. 'I'll never forget my first day of training after I arrived from Motherwell. It was 40 minutes of non-stop running. That was a bit of a shock after Motherwell where if we were playing midweek games, training always tended to be light. Jock didn't believe in easy introductions.'

This was also the time of the famous visits to Gullane sands for pre-season training. 'Conditioning,' Jock Wallace called it. Torture was the verdict of some of the players who still don't like to bring up the subject, since they brought everything up at the time. 'I never had a "yawn" at Gullane,' says Forsyth. 'But wouldn't have recommended anyone having a good breakfast beforehand! We had a great bunch of lads, with a lot of respect for each other. Tommy McLean was a superb player and Alex MacDonald never got the credit he deserved. He put so much work in to help his fellow players.'

Premier Division football came to Scotland in 1975-76. And Rangers celebrated the new arrival by taking that first-ever Premier flag, six points clear of Celtic.

The League Cup was won 1-0 against Celtic because of a diving header from Alex MacDonald. And Hearts were

Here we go again . . . Forsyth
strides out ready for
another day's defensive work.

defeated 3-1 in the Scottish Cup Final, with MacDonald again
a scorer.

After a fallow year in '76-77, Wallace again led his team to
the treble in '77-78. 'These were incredible years for us all,'
recalls Forsyth. And not without funny moments either.

The Ibrox men of that time still speak of the post-mortem
talk that raged on for hours in Willie Waddell's room in a
Hamburg hotel after Rangers had been beaten 3-0 in a game to
mark the 800th year of the City of Glasgow. Finally in the heat
of the night, Forsyth rose to his feet with considerable dignity
and announced: 'I have had enough of this. I don't have to
take this. I can go back to being a joiner.' He then made a
grand exit. Or at least would have done . . . 'except for the fact
I walked into a cupboard instead of out of the door,' says
Tom. 'Boy, did I catch some flak for that one.'

Internationally, he had opened the right door. After
almost a three-year gap following his second cap against
Czechoslovakia in Bratislavia in October 1973, he was recalled
for the game against Switzerland at Hampden on April 7, 1976
. . . and made captain! He led the team to a 1-0 win, and then
had the distinction of playing in a Scottish side that won its

next four games in succession: Wales (3-1), N. Ireland (3-0), England (2-1) and Finland (6-0).

Before the England match of the Channon tackle, there was controversy as then Manchester United manager Tommy Docherty, clearly seeking to promote his own man Martin Buchan in preference to Forsyth, commented that it was 'like comparing a thoroughbred with a Clydesdale'. Which only served to fire up Forsyth. 'I couldn't believe any manager would say that in public. I have never forgotten and wouldn't give Docherty the time of day.'

Forsyth played his part in the memorable qualifying competition for the 1978 World Cup . . . and also the best-forgotten disaster of Argentina that followed. Indeed, the 3-2 win over Holland which came too late to save Scotland was Forsyth's last match in the dark blue jersey.

Injuries were beginning to take a toll, too, and his appearances over the next few seasons became less and less until finally on March 13, 1982 he quit the game on medical advice.

'No regrets,' he says. 'Except I would have liked Rangers to have done better in Europe when I was playing. But I don't think our style was right.

'And I did have the pleasure of playing against Johan Cruyff once. Never laid a glove on him. I couldn't, he was far too fast for me!'

He had a spell as manager of Dunfermline, but that didn't work out. And was delighted to renew the 'Little and Large' act with his close friend Tommy McLean, first with Morton where they took the team into the Premier Division, and now back where it all began at Fir Park.

'I enjoy working with the young players. We have a dozen YTS kids here. But I do feel that Scottish boys are pushed too hard into too many 11-a-side games too quickly. They should be given more scope to play five or six-a-side soccer.'

He can't see any new Jaws on the horizon . . . 'but there are one or two wee Piranhas,' he jokes.

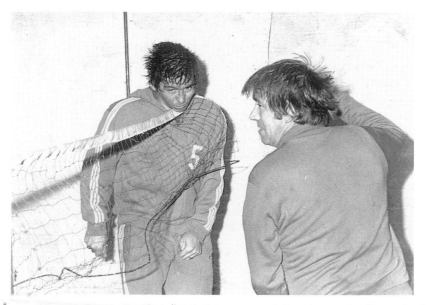

Hang about. Even in the friendly game of heady-tennis Forsyth is committed to win the ball . . . watched by a bemused . . . or is it amused John Greig.

Tom Forsyth's honours:

1971

| June | Denmark | (a) | 0-1 |

1973

| Oct. | Czechoslovakia | (a) | 0-1 |

1976

Apr.	Switzerland	(h)	1-0
May	Wales	(h)	3-1
May	Northern Ireland	(h)	3-0
May	England	(h)	2-1
Sept.	Finland	(h)	6-0

1977

Apr.	Sweden	(h)	3-1
May	Wales	(a)	0-0
June	Northern Ireland	(h)	3-0
June	England	(a)	2-1

1977
(cont'd)

June	Chile	(a)	4-2
June	Argentina	(a)	1-1
June	Brazil	(a)	0-2
Sept.	Czechoslovakia	(h)	3-1
Oct.	Wales	(n)	2-0
	(Played in Liverpool)		

1978

May	Northern Ireland	(h)	1-1
May	Wales (sub)	(h)	1-1
May	England	(h)	0-1
June	Peru	(W.C. Arg)	1-3
June	Iran (sub)	(W.C.)	1-1
June	Holland	(W.C.)	3-2

The day of the long studs. A delirious Tom Forsyth celebrates the famous
goal which earned Rangers the Scottish Cup in the 3-2 win over Celtic in
1973. Joining in is winger Cutty Young.

CHAPTER 8

Davie Cooper

DAVIE COOPER IS NOW IN HIS 18TH YEAR AS A top-line professional footballer. Which is pretty good going for a man who admits to being blatantly one-footed and with a deep loathing of training.

'There is nothing I would have liked better in all my days than to say cheerio to the lads at 4.45 p.m. every Saturday, and not to have seen them again until two o'clock a week later,' says the 35-year-old. 'But I knew it could never be like that. Never at any time did I particularly enjoy training. I could put up with it on warm days, with the sun on my back. But the normal daily grind in our usual conditions . . . I could skip that any time.'

That was never a possibility, of course, and indeed Cooper had to buckle down to the job for many years under the most severe taskmaster of all . . . the formidable Jock Wallace.

But even the legendary Wallace knew when to leave well alone. And while he would like to see Cooper do as much work as the others in training, when it came to games he let the mercurial man the football writers happily dubbed 'The Moody Blue' do his own thing.

Which meant that at times life was frustrating for the Rangers management, the other players and the supporters. For when Cooper was on song . . . the 'music' was a football rhapsody of the kind only the likes of Jim Baxter could produce in his peak. But when he was on an off day, Coop's nonchalant acceptance of the fact went down badly with his

Cooper-man in full flight. He leaves the opposition behind in his testimonial game against French club Bordeaux.

boss, his team-mates and many of the fans who felt if they were not getting inspiration, they would like to see at least some perspiration.

'It used to annoy me when I took a lot more stick than some other players,' says Davie. 'It seems that flair players get more flak than the ordinary worker type of footballer. Guys who aren't expected to do anything out of the ordinary can just play away with no hassle. But I would get laldy for not beating six men. And a lot of this came at a time when for four or five years I was the only international player in the Ibrox team. I have to admit that really bugged me. I couldn't simply wave a wand and produce magic all the time.'

Coop now realises that great expectation is the burden that

is carried along with great talent. 'I would rather be my kind of player than a worker. They're ten a penny,' he says.

Listening to Davie in this kind of expansive mood, you wonder how he ever managed to get himself dubbed the Greta Garbo of Scottish football . . . or 'The Moody Blue' as he was known.

'It really all started long before Rangers, in my days at Clydebank,' says Davie. 'I just didn't fancy the publicity at first, and then Bankies boss Jack Steedman said to me that this was a good gimmick and I should stick to it. When I went to Rangers I opened up a little, but then at one point I decided I was getting a lot of unfair criticism from some of the football writers, so I simply stopped talking to any of them. I thought they were picking on me. And you know it wasn't until I was in the middle of a re-signing dispute with Rangers a few years later that I realised I was wrong. The Press boys came in right behind me and said I was due a better deal.'

There was one other benefit Davie enjoyed because of his reputation: he WAS left alone. 'The fans used to think I was some kind of Howard Hughes and they tended to steer clear of me!' Even the Celtic fans, with whom Cooper was inclined to have a running war.

'I loved the Old Firm games. And I loved beating Celtic. I wasn't just a Rangers player, I was a Rangers MAN. I didn't take any trouble to hide this from the Parkhead support. In fact there was nothing more I enjoyed than teasing them. Boy, did they give me some abuse! But you know, I never had any problems off the field. I think that was because, first of all, they have always respected football ability, and secondly they like players who have club loyalty.'

Not all fans have shown the same appreciation of the way Cooper teases the terracing. 'Some of them actually want you arrested if you give them back a little of their own treatment,' he says. 'I don't suppose I will be able to stop the banter with them at this late stage in my career.'

It was a surprise to many when Davie Cooper parted

Scotland style. Coop leaves another defender in his wake.

company with Rangers in the summer of 1989. Including me. For several times Coop told me that he would finish out his playing career as a Rangers man. But after 13 years and more than 600 games he found the prospect of spending most of a season sitting on the substitutes' bench had little attraction.

'Motherwell came in for me, and their offer of first-team

football was one I couldn't refuse. I had tremendous years of success with Rangers; won everything I could, but I still wanted to play on, and I have no regrets about the move. Mind you, I do think some of the write-ups I was given in my first season at Fir Park were a bit over the top. I was only that good some of the time!'

Cooper's long, medal-strewn career with Rangers was started . . . at the second attempt . . . when he signed from Clydebank in June 1977. Rangers had been one of a host of clubs interested in the Cooper talents as a teenager with Avondale, a local amateur side in his home town of Hamilton. But even then Coop was showing a stubborn, individual streak. One that made him give up football for six months because he was too old to play for Avondale and didn't want to play with anyone but his pals. This despite the fact he had already won Scotland recognition at amateur and youth level. 'Yes, I took the huff because I couldn't get what I wanted,' says Davie.

Luckily for Scottish football, Jack Steedman appeared on the scene. He was boss of Clydebank, the club he owned with brother Charlie, and also ran a highly successful car operation in Glasgow. But he still reckons the best bit of business he ever did was persuading Cooper to join up at Kilbowie. 'Even then I had to do a bit of hard selling,' recalls Jack.

'Clydebank seemed a long way from Hamilton where I was working as an apprentice printer,' says Cooper. 'I didn't fancy the travelling at all, and was still swithering until Jack pulled a master stroke. He slipped me a brown envelope with £300 inside it.' That £300 was the best investment the Steedmans ever made. Not only did they get £100,000 for Cooper from Rangers three seasons later, but they saved for Scottish football a rare talent which might have been lost.

And it wasn't long before the real value of the football gem unearthed by Clydebank became known. In two seasons with Cooper turning on his special talents, Bankies won promotion from the Second Division to the First and then the Premier.

Just some of the items picked up in a career full of glittering prizes.

Cooper's contribution earned him recognition from then Scotland manager Willie Ormond who picked him for a First and Second Division Select side against the Highland League.

Aston Villa wanted him at that point, but the idea of a £65,000 move south didn't appeal to Cooper who has always remained strictly a home bird. Home being Hamilton, for despite the fact that his house is actually in Motherwell, Davie says he couldn't tell you what Motherwell main street looks like!

Rangers' determination to bring Cooper to Ibrox was strengthened by an extraordinary series of League Cup quarter-final games in season 1976-77. A late Cooper goal in the first game at Ibrox meant a 3-3 draw in a match which Davie recalls for the flying lessons he received. 'I was sent flying first of all by John Greig, and then made the return trip by courtesy of Tom Forsyth,' says Coop, who survived the experience to carry on tormenting Rangers in a running battle that took four games to reach a decider.

By June 1977 Cooper was at last a Rangers player in a £100,000 deal that was conducted mainly by telephone since Jack Steedman was on holiday in the South of England. Rangers got a player Clydebank coach Bill Munro described as 'as cheeky as George Best' and new boss Jock Wallace hailed as 'the most exciting prospect in Scottish football'.

New Scotland manager Ally MacLeod took Cooper along in the pre-World Cup fact-finding trip to South America. And although the youngster didn't get to play in any of the games against Chile, Argentina or Brazil, he felt he was really on his way.

'But I began to think again when my first season at Ibrox opened up with two League defeats against Aberdeen at Pittodrie and then Hibs at Ibrox,' recalls Cooper. 'There were actually fans who stayed behind to boo the team after the Hibs game. I took a lot longer to settle than I thought and for the first couple of months I think everyone was wondering if it was all a mistake.'

Seven months later and there were no doubts. For in an incredible first season for Cooper, Rangers swept the board. They won the League Cup by beating Celtic 2-1 at Hampden in March, with a delighted Cooper scoring the first goal in a game that went to extra time. They won the Scottish Cup by beating Aberdeen 2-1 at Hampden on May 6. And they took the

Learning the trade. The teenage Cooper at work as a printer in his home town of Hamilton in his Clydebank days

championship by two points from Aberdeen, having recovered from that shaky start to lose only one of their next 23 League games. Cooper played in 35 of the League games and scored six goals; he was in all eight League Cup ties and scored once, and it was the same in the Scottish Cup.

'What a start. I really thought I had made it and there would be no problems,' says Davie. Wrong.

At the end of that season Jock Wallace unexpectedly left Rangers, and just as unexpectedly John Greig was rocketted straight from the dressing room to the danger room. And that meant problems for Cooper. For Greigy was not entirely sold on the Ibrox new boy despite that first-season success. Playing at left back behind Cooper, it was clear in many games that Greig was looking for a lot more hard work from the man in front of him.

'I think he felt I was not so much laid back, more inclined to lying down,' recalls Davie. 'Greigy was one of the blood, sweat and tears brigade. I like to win as much as the next man. But I like to do it with a bit of style.'

Jock Wallace, who certainly didn't like shirkers, was prepared to put up with cool Coop. 'At one point he did try to make me use my right foot more and banned me from using my left for a week in training,' recalls Cooper. 'But when he saw that I would rather HEAD the ball than use my right he gave up!'

Cooper won two more Cup medals in Greig's first season: victory by 2-1 over Aberdeen in the League Cup and 3-2 against Hibs in a Scottish Cup Final that ran longer than some West End plays. It needed three games and two sessions of extra time before Rangers succeeded after five and a half hours of less than riveting football.

'But it was clear I was by no means a favourite of the manager,' says Davie. 'I was left out of most of the club's European ties that season, with the view expressed that I was not the right kind of player for that kind of tactical battle.' Cooper started in only 41 of the team's 55 competitive games; was used as substitute seven times and taken off and replaced in a dozen other matches. 'Not the happiest of times for me' says Davie. 'I had to keep reassuring myself I was still a good player, but there is no doubt I became a bit sloppy in the years under John Greig.'

Before Greig departed in October 1983, a saddened and frustrated man, Cooper had added two more medals to his

Reaching for success. Cooper stretches out the famous left foot as he goes for goal in a game against Airdrie.

collection . . . both at the expense of Dundee United. And it was the 4-1 replay victory in the 1981 Scottish Cup Final that gave Cooper probably the most satisfaction of any game of his entire career. And just to show what a funny game football can be, he only got the chance for this golden game because of a missed penalty.

'Myself and big Derek Johnstone were left out of the Final team in the first game which finished up 0-0,' says Davie.

'And if Ian Redford hadn't missed a penalty in the last minute, there wouldn't have been that chance for me in the replay. I was determined to prove the point that I should have been in from the start. I think I did.'

He did indeed. It was Cooper who set the jamboree going with the opening goal in 10 minutes. And he proceeded to destroy what was acknowledged to be one of the best defences in the country . . . to such an extent that before half an hour had gone he had laid on two more goals for Bobby Russell and John MacDonald as Rangers swept to a 4-1 triumph.

There are many people who believe that this was Cooper's

finest hour (well, 90 minutes to be more accurate) in a Rangers jersey. Cooper being Cooper is inclined to argue.

'I think my first Old Firm game at Ibrox on September 10, 1977 takes some beating. We let big Shuggie Edvaldsson through to score twice in the first half and were 2-0 down at the interval. I'll never forget big Jock Wallace saying to us: "You have let them score two shitty goals, you had better get back out there and score three good ones." We did!'

But of all the games and all the goals that the magic left foot conjured up, it is the one he netted in the 1979 Drybrough Cup Final. 'Fortunately enough, I was later presented with it on a video . . . and I still enjoy watching it,' says Davie. 'The fact that it was against Celtic makes it even more pleasant.' Cooper took down a cross from Alex MacDonald, flicked the ball up and over Celtic centre-half Roddy MacDonald, and dazzled both Murdo MacLeod and Tom McAdam before flicking the ball in the air again over Alan Sneddon, then firing it past Peter Latchford. All done with the left foot, naturally!

Cooper got the first of his 22 Scottish Caps against Peru at Hampden in the 1-1 draw in September 1979, and was brought on as substitute against Austria a month later in another 1-1 game. But then there is a long gap until his next dark blue appearance . . . against Wales in the 2-1 victory at Hampden in February 1984.

The reason for his lack of dark blue jerseys was his moody blue image. 'I should have had more caps. But for a number of years I just lost interest. It was sheer stubborness, I guess.' It took a double dose of Jock-talk to bring the wandering star back into line. 'When Jock Wallace arrived back at Ibrox I was overweight and sluggish. He gave me a month to take off five pounds . . . I did it in a week,' says Davie.

That was in November 1983. By February 1984 Cooper was back in the Scotland line-up under Jock Stein. He played and scored (from the penalty spot) in the 2-1 win over Wales . . . a game where a certain golden-haired boy from Watford was making his international debut. Mo Johnston!

Sporting a new line in training gear . . . Coop was a great believer in using a plastic bin bag to help lose weight in his pre-season training.

Cooper's cap career didn't exactly flourish after that: his total of 22 is paltry for a player of such ability. He was seldom used in away games, confirming his own feeling that players of his particular individual style are regarded as luxury items. 'Or maybe like some vintage wines we don't travel well,' he jokes.

And his most significant contribution in all his games was lost in the gloom of Jock Stein's death. Scotland needed a

point to ensure a play-off place against Australia when they
faced the Welsh at Cardiff on September 10, 1985. Cooper got
it for them, coming off the substitutes' bench to strike home
the vital 80th-minute penalty that brought a 1-1 draw.

'Putting me on for Gordon Strachan was probably Jock
Stein's last footballing move,' says Davie. 'It wasn't worth
losing a man like that for a game of football. He was my kind
of manager: he simply told me to get out there and do what I
was good at.'

By the time Cooper got to Mexico with Scotland for the
World Cup, he was in the company of his new boss . . . Graeme
Souness having joined Rangers in April 1986 as player-
manager. 'I really didn't get to play alongside him as much as I
would have liked because he soon concentrated on just being a
manager rather than a player. And I regret that. He was a
superb footballer, but a bit of a frightener, too. They used to
say how good he was at making space for himself, but I think a
lot of people were just glad to leave him alone! Others tried,
and came out of the clash with the silver medal.'

It was Souness who set up the pay day that ensured
Cooper would be comfortable for life. 'When we were in
Mexico for the World Cup he asked how many years I had been
at Ibrox. When I told him he said I was due a testimonial
match, and when I told him they had been stopped, he replied:
"That'll be right".' So it came about that on the 9th of August
1988 some 44,000 fans turned out in tribute as Rangers played
French club Bordeaux in the Davie Cooper Testimonial . . .
with another 5,000 locked out.

They might not have shown it all the time, but the fans
proved that night just how much they respected the talents of
the Moody Blue.

Cooper played more than 600 games for Rangers; he was
in three Scottish Cup-winning teams; he won seven League Cup
medals and was in three championship-lifting teams. He left
Ibrox only because of the lure of first-team football at Fir Park
under former colleague Tommy McLean, whom he admired as
a player and now as a manager.

Just a boy. Davie Cooper takes the field in his early days at Ibrox.

But he is no lover of Premier Division football. 'It's a skill killer,' he declares. 'There appears to be no room for the flair player. Only six-foot athletes who can run and kick. If I hadn't been such a home bird I would have moved elsewhere. But surely the warning signs are there when players like Gary McAllister prefer to stay clear of the Premier League set-up, preferring to stay in England with Leeds rather than come back North.'

He is no admirer, either, of Scottish referees, a feeling which can hardly have escaped many since the bulk of Cooper's bookings have been for telling the referee how to do his job. 'I feel it's someone's duty to tell them,' he says. 'I really believe we have to turn to full-time professional refs in the future. Most of the current crop are like schoolteachers, and treat you like a pupil. You can't talk to many of them. Kenny Hope is an exception. I remember telling him in my usual fashion in one game that I thought he was having a stinker and he reminded me I wasn't playing so well myself.'

Unfortunately, there is little chance of Cooper staying on in football to pass on his special skills. 'I don't have the patience for coaching,' he says. 'You can either play or you can't. When I finish up in football, I fancy running a wee restaurant. It will be in Hamilton, naturally!'

Davie Cooper's honours:

1980

Sept.	Peru	(h)	1-1
Oct.	Austria (sub)	(h)	1-1

1984

Feb.	Wales	(h)	2-1
May	England	(h)	1-1
Sept.	Yugoslavia	(h)	6-1
Oct.	Northern Ireland	(h)	3-0

1985

Feb.	Spain	(a)	0-1
Mar.	Wales	(h)	0-1
Sept.	Wales	(a)	1-1
Oct.	East Germany	(h)	0-0
Nov.	Australia	(h)	2-0
Dec.	Australia	(a)	0-0

1986

Apr.	Holland	(a)	0-0
June	West Germany (sub)	(W.C.)	1-2
June	Uruguay (sub)	(W.C.)	0-0
Sept.	Bulgaria	(h)	0-0
Nov.	Luxembourg	(h)	3-0

1987

Feb.	Republic of Ireland	(h)	0-1
May	Brazil	(h)	0-2

1989

Nov.	Norway	(h)	1-1

1990

May	Egypt	(h)	1-3

Cooper also played in Scotland's very first Under-21 match against Czechoslovakia in 1977 as a Clydebank player. He won six Under-21 honours.

CHAPTER 9

Terry Butcher

BIG TERRY BUTCHER LEFT SCOTLAND WITH regret . . . and would return with alacrity. But only if he were handed Graeme Souness' job!

The former Rangers and England captain, now player-boss of English First Divsion side Coventry, has fulfilled a lifetime ambition by becoming a manager. And he is happy to be back in his native country. But he would gladly have stayed on in Scotland where he and his family had settled easily.

'The trouble is, after being with Rangers I simply cannot see myself being content with another club in Scotland. Rangers are the biggest club in the country. Anything after them would be a let down, I'm sure. And since I can't imagine the Scottish F.A. offering me the national team job, the only one that looks tempting is at Ibrox.

'The trouble is, I don't think Graeme Souness wants to give it up!'

Which is why Butcher took the low road south in the winter of 1990 following a well-publicised bust-up between himself and Souness, the man who brought this larger-than-life personality into Scottish football. El Tel has refused to become El Tell, and jump on the lolly lorry to reveal his side of the sad affair. And might never. He has respect for Souness; more for the club; and a lot more still for the Rangers supporters.

'My time north of the border was never anything less than eventful.' he says. 'There was hardly a dull moment. When I decided to go north I wondered what life would be like as an

Riding high. Terry celebrates a League Championship triumph . . . ably assisted by Richard Gough and Chris Woods.

Englishman living in Scotland. Now I know. Bloody interesting!

'My wife Rita and my three sons adapted well to living in Scotland. We had a superb way of life; a lovely home in a beautiful part of the country with the magnificent scenery of the Highlands just a short drive away. And we were made welcome not only by Rangers fans, but by the many friends we gained in our time in Scotland. It was a hard decision to make when the time came for us to leave. And one of our main jobs when house-hunting in Coventry was to get a place that was first of all high enough so I didn't bang my head on the low rafters that are so common in the area . . . and secondly had enough room to accommodate all our Scottish friends who say they'll be visiting us.'

But there were undoubtedly times when the 6ft 4in Butcher wondered if his journey north was really necessary. Or wise. Every time triumph strolled through the door, controversy came tagging along behind. Usually to find the door bearing the famous Butcher trademark (a severe dent!).

In his first few years at Ibrox Butcher had the heady success of three League championships and three successive Skol Cup victories. But he had also had a broken leg; been dragged through the courts for his part in the infamous Old Firm punch-up in October 1987; been fined £500 by the S.F.A. for bringing the game into disrepute when he kicked the referee's door after a game at Pittodrie; and been caught in the act by the TV cameras when he almost removed the door from its hinges at Parkhead after the Scottish Cup defeat in 1990.

Jokes about Terry and doors have multiplied over the years. And he cannot quite fathom himself why he has this penchant for punishing the woodwork. 'It's not a new thing. I did damage to a door or two in my days at Ipswich,' he says. 'I guess it's just sheer frustration. But, anyway, surely it's better that I take out my feelings on the door rather than someone else? I do take a bit of stick about it. There have been suggestions that my personal sponsors are B & Q! The time

Cheers all the way as Terry brandishes the League Championship trophy aloft.

when I was caught in the candid camera shot at Parkhead, I knew nothing about it. I never saw the photographer and reporter standing there interviewing Billy McNeill.

'I had stayed on the pitch to congratulate the Celtic players on their win. But the run from the pitch up the tunnel at Parkhead is long. And it's exposed. By the time I made it indoors I had been given a right load of abuse, and worse, from some supporters, so I was boiling. When I got home to Dunblane I slipped down for a quiet pint at the local . . . and was given more stick from my friends. I couldn't understand at first how they knew about it . . . until they told me the whole country had witnessed my spectacular exit.'

Celtic fans in particular relish making the most of Butcher's door fetish. Sitting in the Parkhead press box after one recent Old Firm game — the writers are out in the open air and can pick up the comments of the spectators — I can recall the cry that went up as the Rangers captain headed for the dressing room after a defeat: 'Is there a joiner in the house?' one Parkhead punter demanded!

Yet Butcher has no complaints about the Celtic fans: 'I never found them any less friendly than any others,' he says. 'Of course, they're happier if they've won. But who isn't?'

I suspect the Celtic supporters recognised in Butcher the kind of committed team player they enjoy seeing in a green and white jersey. Butcher is fiercely competitive, and puts such concentration into a game that for 90 minutes he sees nothing else. Yet when it is over, he is the first man to go to the fans and express his appreciation. Pictures of Butcher in hats and scarves abound after victory: he is inundated with requests to visit supporters' clubs and always has time to stop and talk with the supporters.

When England battled through to the semi-finals of the 1990 World Cup in Italy, it was Butcher and Chris Waddle who led the singing and dancing in front of the supporters at the end of the games. He is a punter's player: always will be. Even in his long career with Ipswich, starting as a teenager, Terry was always a fan favourite. He responded to this by sticking with the Suffolk club through good times and bad for nine years.

Terry was a local lad made good. But he was actually born in Singapore in December, 1958 while his father was serving with the Royal Navy. The Butcher family moved back to home territory at Lowestoft in Suffolk, and it was there the Butcher boy began to show his talent for football. He was recommended as a schoolboy to local club Ipswich by the secretary of the Lowestoft branch of the supporters' club and taken on by then Ipswich boss Bobby Robson — later to be his international team manager — and was in the youth team in 1976-77. He quickly went on to the reserves and then the first team, hastened all the way by the ruthless reserve coach Bobby Ferguson, who was convinced Butcher had what it took . . . but was too nice.

Wounded warrior. Butcher goes into action in typical style despite a heavily protected wound.

Imagine big Terry as a feartie! 'Pansy' was one of the nicer words used by the Ipswich coach to the gangling youngster. It was tough stuff, but the end result of Ferguson's haranguing was a totally determined, dedicated professional who only wants to be a winner . . . whatever team he happens to be playing with.

By the time Graeme Souness made his move for Butcher in the summer of 1986, Butcher had progressed from raw boy through the ranks to captain of Ipswich and full internationalist. But in nine years at Portman Road he had only one medal to show for it — from the 1981 U.E.F.A. Cup when Ipswich beat Dutch team AZ Alkmaar. He had played nearly 400 first-team games for Ipswich when decision time came in the summer of 1986. Terry had signed a new three-year contract with the club, which included a clause which agreed to sell him if Ipswich were relegated from the First Division.

'I didn't think that could happen. But it did. And I knew it was time to go,' says Butcher. But go where? Manchester United were ready to bid . . . but didn't. Chelsea were interested . . . but didn't follow through. Tottenham Hotspur were keen, but not keen enough to pay the money Ipswich wanted.

And then there was Rangers. New Ibrox boss Graeme Souness had arrived as player-manager just a few weeks before both England and Scotland set out for Mexico in the World Cup. And it was while both were in Mexico as players that the moves began.

'I was flattered when I heard Rangers wanted me. But it still didn't seem likely I would go to Scotland. I didn't know much about the football up there, but I had learned what their fans thought about the English!'

There was also the slight problem that as a player, Butcher was one of many who detested the arrogant way Souness ran the game for Liverpool and was in the queue of those who would like to have knocked a little of the swagger out of him. Many tried. Few succeeded . . . and others were left with a painful reminder of the price of failure.

Who's a happy skipper then? Terry shows just how he feels after scoring against Motherwell. Moving in to join him are Mo Johnston and Ally McCoist.

Souness pursued his man all the way, persuaded him to come up to Glasgow to see around Ibrox, and offered Ipswich £750,000 . . . more money than anyone else. So Terry Butcher, captain of Ipswich (and shortly to skipper England as well), became captain of Rangers: assured by his new manager that 'the fans will treat you like a God'.

And sure enough, when Butcher made his debut in a friendly against Arsenal at Ibrox on August 5, 1986 he was astonished at the welcome he received from 36,300 fans. 'And even though we lost 2-0 they still cheered me all the way. I couldn't believe it'.

His credulity was stretched again four days later in his very next game, his competitive debut against Hibs at Easter Road. The new-look Rangers, with Butcher, Chris Woods, Colin

West and Souness himself playing in a Premier game for the very first time, not only lost the game. They lost the place, as did Hibs. This followed a wild Souness tackle that felled George McCluskey and brought about a mélée that was eventually to lead the S.F.A. to punish every player on the field — with the exception of home goalkeeper Alan Rough, who typically felt it was too much bother to run halfway up the pitch to get involved.

Souness was sent off. Butcher was later booked and ultimately he and 20 other players were docked another two penalty points. Butcher was perplexed. It was like being invited to a party which finished up with all the guests mugging each other. 'I soon discovered that, with Rangers, there was no such thing as a dull day or an ordinary game,' he says. 'Every week brought something different'.

Something different included medals. In his very first season Butcher beefed up his medal collection from one to three. He laid his hands on his first trophy as Rangers captain by taking the Skol Cup at Hampden on October 26, 1986. And since the success was achieved against Old Firm rivals Celtic, the big Englishman was established as an instant legend.

But, again, it was no ordinary affair. Referee Davie Syme booked TEN players and ordered one off . . . Mo Johnston OF CELTIC!

The trophy was won on a disputed penalty.

'Well, Celtic disputed it. But I thought it was a clear award,' says Terry. He was certainly in a position to know . . . it was given after he had been blocked in the area by his Celtic counterpart Roy Aitken as they both went for a free kick.

Davie Cooper slotted in the spot kick for victory, with Ian Durrant having already scored for Rangers and Brian McClair equalising.

A crowd of 74,219 watched that dramatic affair. The teams were:

Celtic — Bonner; Grant, MacLeod; Aitken, Whyte, McGhee (Archdeacon); McClair, McStay, Johnston, Shepherd, McInally.

New strip. New club. Same old Butcher. Terry in action as player-manager at Coventry.

Rangers — Woods, Nicholl, Munro; Fraser (MacFarlane), Dawson, Butcher; D. Ferguson, McMinn, McCoist (Fleck), Durrant, Cooper.

The celebrations lasted well into the night, and only the keen eye of manager Graeme Souness prevented the kind of

Moment of agony. Terry is carried off by physio Phil Boersma and team-mate Stuart Munro after breaking his leg against Aberdeen.

incident that was to become notorious in Rugby when the Calcutta Cup was taken on an 'excursion' in Edinburgh and finished up damaged. Butcher was heading out the door at Ibrox with the trophy, bound for a party, when Souness spotted him and gave the Cup over to someone he clearly felt was far more responsible at that point . . . one of the groundstaff!

Terry missed only one game in that first season, and by the end of it had his hands on another trophy . . . the League championship. Halfway through the season that didn't look a prospect: Rangers trailed Celtic by eight points after losing 1-0 to Aberdeen at Pittodrie in a game where Davie McPherson was sent off. But a 3-0 home win over Hearts on November 29 set Rangers off on a run that was to bring them 16 wins and three draws in the next 19 games. As they found a new gear, Celtic were slipping into reverse.

However, Butcher was learning that making a drama out of a crisis was the norm with Rangers. They went to Pittodrie in the second last game of the season knowing a draw would be good enough to give them the title. They got it. But not before player-manager Souness had made the referee see red for the

Above them all. Terry rises high as he goes into action against Hibs.

second time that season and was in the shower before half-time. Despite being down to 10 men, Rangers took the lead . . . with a Terry Butcher header. And although Dons equalised, the news came through that Celtic had lost at home to Falkirk.

'And that started the biggest party I have ever been at,' says Butcher. His feet literally never touched the ground . . . instead he was carted round the stadium in triumph by delirious fans.

Family man. Terry and his wife Rita.

It was an incredible first season for Butcher, topped off by one of the most unusual events in Scottish international football. He played against Scotland at Hampden. And the game finished 0-0. What's so different about that? Well there were more Rangers players in the England side than the Scottish team: Woods and Butcher lining up for England and only McCoist for Scotland!

By the time Butcher left Ibrox, the dressing room was awash with a variety of English accents . . . Woods, Stevens, Vinnicombe, Steven, Butcher, Spackman, Walters, Hateley, Hurlock. The irrepressible Ally McCoist summed it up in one match. An angry opponent, dumped unceremoniously by one of the Sassenachs, got to his feet bellowing: 'You dirty English bastard, I'll get you.' To which McCoist replied: 'Which of the English bastards are you talking about? There's seven of them out here.'

Butcher's first season was a triumph: his second a catalogue of disaster. He missed the start of season '87-88

Not so little drummer boy. In his spare time Terry enjoys giving the cymbals a rattle.

because of suspension; was laid up with a back injury; was ordered off against Celtic in the infamous 2-2 game at Ibrox along with Chris Woods and Frank McAvennie and which led to him being charged with conduct liable to cause a breach of the peace. And subsequently fined £250 in court. Then on November 17, in a home game against Aberdeen, he broke his leg trying to get in a shot as Alex McLeish blocked the ball. A lesser man might have cut and run for the border at that point. But Butcher is a big man in all ways. 'I felt I had done nothing wrong. I wasn't going to run away.'

He never played again that season, but by 1988-89 was back . . . and back in bother, too, because of his liking for re-arranging the shape of doors. In the game at Pittodrie on October 8 when Ian Durrant was carried off with a horrific injury, Butcher took out his frustration on a dressing-room door again. Unfortunately it led to the referee's room and the incident was witnessed by police who charged him with vandalism and breach of the peace. 'I thought: here we go again,' says Terry. But this time there was to be no court appearance, just a lot of bad publicity and a £500 fine from the S.F.A. for miscounduct.

Once again, Butcher showed tremendous strength of character and buckled down to the job of leading Rangers to another Skol Cup Final in the thrilling 3-2 Hampden victory over Aberdeen; had the League championship won three matches from the end of the season; and had the coveted treble in sight.

All that was needed was to dispose of Celtic in the Scottish Cup Final. But over-confidence and a slip in front of goal by Gary Stevens put paid to that dream as Joe Miller pounced on the error for the only goal of the game. 'We should have known better. Old Firm games are different from anything I've ever known. You know things are settling down when the pace drops to 100 miles an hour. The football is so often attrocious in these games because there's so much at stake. These games take over your life for a week before they're played — and a week after if you win. Four of them in a season is quite enough, I think.'

There was one more League title for Butcher to savour before setting out for the World Cup in Italy, where he was to share in England's good and sad moments, winning the last of his 77 caps (32 of them with Rangers), Rangers took the title easily, losing only five games and finishing up with 51 points . . . seven clear of second-placed Aberdeen. Butcher missed only two games, and was inspirational as he marshalled a defence that conceded only 19 goals in 34 games compared to the 33 lost by Dons, who incidentally scored 56 against Rangers' 48.

Butcher seemed set in cement at Ibrox. But unexpectedly cracks appeared. First of all he had to have a close-season knee operation, and combined with his World Cup exertions was ill at ease and lacked timing in his opening matches of the new season. A spectacular own goal in the 2-1 defeat by Dundee United at Tannadice on September 22, 1990 was followed by the unthinkable: Butcher was bulleted.

A pair of Sassenachs who won over the Rangers fans . . . Butcher and Mark Walters.

Manager Souness was of the opinion that the big defender had not made his way back to full fitness after his operation and World Cup exertions. He was sent on a solo get-fit programme. Not quite sent to Coventry . . . but as it turned out that was to follow within a few months.

But not before a celebrated bust-up after the 2-1 Skol Cup Final victory over Celtic where it was revealed that Butcher had been asked to make a comeback because of the injury situation at Ibrox . . . but declined, believing it would not be right for himself or the club.

At this point, as they say in Glasgow: 'Yer tea's oot'. Which roughly translated means: 'You've have had it pal'. Indeed not only was Butcher's tea 'oot' . . . so was he. Within weeks he was back in his native England. But not before one final piece of drama. He was expected to join Leeds as a player, but unexpectedly produced a dainty body swerve for such a big man and ended up in Coventry as player-boss.

Butcher's sojourn in Scotland might have been comparatively short: but it was certainly sweet. In the space of 176 games for Rangers he managed to win three League medals and two Skol Cups as well as 32 caps for his country, which just goes to prove that civilisation does not stop at the border. Well, not going north it doesn't.!'

Butcher's advice to any young Englishman is: go north young man, if you get the chance.

But for God's sake take your tin helmet!

Terry Butcher's honours:

1980
Australia

1981
Spain

1982
Wales
Scotland
France
Czechoslovakia
West Germany
Spain

1983
Denmark
West Germany
Luxembourg
Wales
Greece
Holland
Northern Ireland
Scotland
Australia (3)

1984
Denmark
Hungary
Luxembourg
France
Northern Ireland

1985
East Germany
Finland
Turkey
Northern Ireland
Republic of Ireland
Romania
Finland
Scotland
Italy
West Germany
United States

1986
Israel
Russia
Scotland
Mexico
Canada
Portugal
Morocco
Poland
Paraguay
Argentina

The following caps were won after he joined Rangers:

1987
Sweden
Northern Ireland (2)
Yugoslavia
Spain
Brazil
Scotland

1988
Turkey
Yugoslavia

1989
Denmark
Sweden
Greece
Albania (2)
Czechoslovakia
Scotland
Poland
Denmark

1990
Sweden
Poland
Italy
Yugoslavia
Brazil
Czechoslovakia
Denmark
Uruguay
Tunisia
Republic of Ireland
Holland
Belgium
Cameroons
West Germany

CHAPTER 10

Richard Gough

RICHARD GOUGH HAD A CHOICE OF COUNTRIES where he could pursue an international career. He was born in Sweden, lived as a child in England, then spent most of his life in South Africa . . . but is very much a Scot like his father. And nothing has given him more pleasure than joining the exclusive 50-cap club for his country.

Except that his pleasure was blunted by the fact that he only lasted until half-time in the game that counted. He came off at half-time in the World Cup tie against Costa Rica and was sitting on the bench when the Central American side scored the goal that was ultimately to knock Scotland out of the competition. 'So I'm probably in an exclusive club with membership limited to one — the forty-nine-and-a-half cap club!' he jokes.

Richard Charles Gough was born in the Swedish capital Stockholm on April 5, 1962. His Swedish mother Lisa met and married his father Charlie in Aldershot, where Gough senior was stationed as a paratrooper. 'My mother did the traditional thing — she went home to her mother to have her first baby,' says Richard. 'The Swedish press made a lot of this during the World Cup since their team was in the same section as us, but I'm afraid my knowledge of the language is practically zero. My father bought himself out of the paratroop regiment in 1965 and we moved to South Africa. He was a footballer, and wanted to play out there. He liked it. We settled. And my brother Jamie and sister Nina were born there.'

Football, and Scottish football especially, was very much an influence in the Gough household. 'The place was always full of former Scottish players like Joe Gilroy, Craig Watson and Bobby Hume. The last two were ex-Rangers players, and I loved listening to their stories about Ibrox. Right from the start I wanted to be a footballer. And I wanted to play with Rangers.'

It looked as though his dream had been realised when in 1980 another former Rangers man, the legendary Don 'Rhino' Kichebrand fixed teenager Gough up with a trial at Ibrox. 'Don worked in the same printing and stationery company as my father. And he urged me to go to Scotland and take a chance.'

But that first visit to Ibrox didn't work out.

'I had one trial game, against Queen's Park at Lesser Hampden, and was told by the manager at the time, John Greig, that unfortunately he couldn't use me since he had enough central defenders.' Greig, now back at Ibrox as public relations executive, undoubtedly winces when he thinks about that decision. It was to cost his club a million and a half pounds seven years later.

That was how much it cost Graeme Souness to bring Gough back to Ibrox. By then the player was in English football with Tottenham, where he had been made club captain after a £750,000 move from Dundee United.

'It really was a case of third time lucky,' says Richard. 'When Graeme Souness arrived at Ibrox at the end of the 1986 season, one of the first things he did was to make an offer for me to Dundee United. But there was no way Jim McLean was going to sell me to another Scottish club if he could help it. He was utterly determined on that. Just as he's stubborn about many things, even when he's in the wrong.'

Gough is well qualified to talk about the highly individualistic style of management at Tannadice. He spent six years there after being shown the door at Ibrox. 'I could have gone back to South Africa, and returned to Witz University to pursue another career. But I wanted to be a footballer. United offered me a chance. And I took it gladly.

Poised for action . . . Richard Gough has that typical determined look about him.

'And I must say Tannadice was a great training ground for any young player. I might not have gone as far as I have without the experience and teaching of Jim McLean. I'm grateful to him for that. But that doesn't mean to say I like him. He was a hard man for anyone to get on with.' Gough, too, is a determined individual. And there were quite a few 'spats' between the pair in his six-year stint at Tannadice.

Gough had made the first team by the end of the 1981 season, coming on as a substitute in a 3-2 defeat by Celtic at Tannadice. But in the December of that year, with Scotland in the grip of a drenching wet, freezing winter which badly affected football, the young Gough was hit by a bout of homesickness and walked out on United.

'I spent nearly two months lounging around in the Johannesburg sunshine and was contemplating giving up football and staying on in South Africa, even though it meant I would have had to do national service in the Army. But Jim McLean kept in touch with my father, who eventually persuaded me to go back. When I did return seven weeks later the weather had been so bad I had missed only one match. So I had definitely wintered in the right place.'

The break obviously sorted out a lot of things in the mind of the young Gough. For he quickly settled down to establishing himself as a key figure in a Dundee United team which had emerged as a major force in Scottish football. United had won the League Cup twice going into the 1980s, and were pipped for a hat-trick of success when Rangers beat them 2-1 in the '81-82 competition. The Tayside team also had some great runs in Europe and to Hampden for Scottish Cup Finals.

'But undoubtedly the best memory of my years at Tannadice was when we astonished everyone by winning the Premier Division title in 1983,' says Richard. 'Aberdeen had emerged as a challenge to Celtic and Rangers for the championship, but no one expected us to beat them all to it.' But they did — by a point from Celtic. And to make victory

The Cup that cheers. Gough, wearing a jersey kindly donated by a defeated Englishman, brandishes aloft the Rous Cup . . . won at Hampden in 1985 thanks to a Gough goal.

sweeter for United, they clinched the title by winning it against their city rivals Dundee at Dens Park.

At Tannadice, Gough operated at right back simply because there was no way United would split up the central defensive pairing of Narey and Hegarty. And there are many people — United's Paul Sturrock for a start — who believe that this is his best position. 'This allows him more freedom to come forward — and he is a great example of the defensive player who threatens to score every time he appears in the opposition box,' says Paul, now coach at Tannadice.

And it was certainly at right back that he won the first of his Scottish honours — in an under-21 international against East Germany at Tynecastle on October 12, 1982 when Scotland won 2-0 with a side which included Steve Nicol, Eric Black, Paul McStay, and Charlie Nicholas.

Two more winning under-21 games later (against Switzerland and Belgium away) and the young Gough was launched on his full international career. He was at right back in the Scotland side which drew 2-2 with Switzerland at Hampden on March 30, 1983. The team was: Leighton; Gough, F. Gray; Souness, Hansen, Miller, Wark, Strachan, Nicholas, Weir. 'It was a first cap for Charlie Nicholas as well,' recalls Richard. 'He played well and scored. I will never understand why a player of his ability never won more caps.'

Gough won 26 caps while at United, as well as a total of five Under-21 honours. But in the build-up to the 1986 World Cup in Mexico he decided it was time to get out of Tannadice. His determination to leave was fired by a half-million pound bid by new Rangers manager Graeme Souness on April 19, 1986. This was refused. So was a subsequent offer of £650,000.

'It was clear Jim McLean would never sell me to Rangers, but I was just as determined to leave. When I returned from the World Cup in 1986 with nothing settled, I told the club I would not turn out in the opening game against Aberdeen in the new season unless they agreed to sell me if a suitable offer came. That caused a fair bit of hassle with Jim McLean, but

Lean, hard and hungry . . . Gough combines 6ft of muscle with athleticism.

eventually it was agreed and after three games of the season I was phoned by director George Grant on the Saturday night of August 16 to say a £750,000 deal had been set up with Spurs.'

Ironically, Gough's last game for United was against Rangers at Ibrox. And it turned out that 13 months later his next game in the Premier Division was FOR Rangers against United at Tannadice.

'I enjoyed my short spell at Tottenham. They were a side packed with talent. It was an experience to play alongside guys likes Ossie Ardiles, Chris Waddle and Glenn Hoddle. I played in the 1987 English Cup Final; made the semi-final of the Littlewoods Cup; and finished third in the League. I had been made captain and signed a year's extension to my contract. But unforseen family circumstances meant I just couldn't settle and I told manager David Pleat that I would like to go back north if the chance came.'

Enter Graeme Souness, who is nothing if not a determined man. It cost him £1.5 million to get his man at the third attempt. 'I flew up to Edinburgh on a Friday morning and was signed by lunch-time', says Richard. He had completed the circle . . . and it was magic.

The Rangers aim was to pair Gough up in the centre of defence with the inspiring Terry Butcher. But the best-laid plans of mice and managers can easily go astray. In his first three games Gough helped beat Dundee United; scored in a 2-2 draw against Celtic; and won a Skol Cup medal in the penalty shoot-out against Aberdeen at Hampden after the teams had drawn 3-3. A dream start for the new firm of Gough and Butcher. But the fourth game became a nightmare.

Butcher broke his leg against Aberdeen on November 17 and was out of football for months. 'That definitely unsettled the side, and there was a lot of coming and going with players as Graeme Souness searched for the right blend,' says Richard.

Rangers finished 12 points adrift of Celtic in the League that season. But the restoration of the Gough-Butcher partnership for 1988-89 changed all that. Gough missed only

In full stride . . . Gough takes to the field in his usual no-nonsense approach.

one League game and Butcher two as Rangers took the title by six points from Aberdeen with Celtic a further four points away. The Skol Cup was taken as well, with a 3-2 Hampden victory over Aberdeen again.

There was a chance of a treble. But Celtic, against the odds, spoiled the expected party by deservedly winning the Scottish Cup with a Joe Miller goal. 'We didn't play well that day. They did,' says Gough.

The 1989-90 was won as well, so in three seasons Gough had two championship medals and two Skol Cup badges. 'And there's more to come,' he says with confidence. 'Graeme Souness is so ambitious he will make sure of this. His arrival turned Scottish football upside down. Other clubs are now having to compete with him in the transfer market, and this in turn is making it harder and harder for us in every game. Not that there is ever such a thing as an easy match playing for Rangers. Even small sides seem to find something extra in their determination to knock us over.'

'I have played against the biggest clubs in England, and Rangers are bigger than them by a mile.'

Which is why in the summer of 1990, just before going off to the World Cup in Italy, Gough signed a new six-year contract with Rangers. The club value him as much as he rates them.

Gough is a strapping six foot of muscle and gristle. A hard player, but fair. But he is no iron man as several injuries have proved. A smashed cheek bone put him out of action for a couple of months in '88-89. 'That was a frustrating injury. I felt fit enough to play after about a month and was training, but wasn't allowed to play.' His next injury was even more frustrating. A mystery damage to the nerve in his big toe of his right foot has meant several operations. But it re-appeared during the World Cup game against Costa Rica, and limited Gough to half a game on his 50th cap occasion.

There was talk of the injury threatening his career, but he dismisses that as 'rubbish'. 'There's a lot to do yet for Rangers

Just champion. Richard celebrates another title triumph with goalkeeper
Chris Woods and fellow defender Terry Butcher . . . who is sporting a new
line in daft hats.

and Scotland,' he says. 'For the club, the big thing would be to
win the European Cup. I know that is one of the manager's
ambitions, having done it himself in his Liverpool days. There
are so many quality teams and players in Europe that it would
be a mammoth task. But not impossible if the draw fell kindly.
We would have to play to our absolute limit as well.'

Gough shows the hard-eyed approach which has won him more than 50 caps for Scotland.

Only one winner . . . Richard Gough rises to clear despite the determined effort of Dunfermline's Ross Jack.

Gough has had his highlights: the championship win with Dundee United; the trophies with Rangers; and of course the memorable extra-time game for Scotland against Cyprus in the World Cup qualifying game.

'Even when we were 2-1 down I still felt we could win,' he says. 'And after I got the equaliser I was even more conviced. But I had no idea how long the referee had let the game run when I went in to meet Roy Aitken's cross at the end of the game. I just knew I was going to score the minute I took off. It wasn't until later I learned that it really was a great escape, and that winner had come six minutes into injury time.'

There have been disappointments too. On a personal basis, his marriage failed. And in football he has had the frustration of being in two World Cup Final campaigns that have also failed. 'And losing to Celtic at Hampden in the 1989 Cup Final when we were going for the treble was a sore one,' he says.

But he firmly believes there are triple times ahead for Rangers. And he wants not just to SHARE them, but to LEAD the way. He was always looked upon as a future Rangers captain. And he was the logical choice when the inspirational Terry Butcher departed. And already he has had the pleasure of holding aloft the Skol Cup Trophy . . . a moment made even sweeter by the fact that victory in the 1990 Final at Hampden was achieved over traditional rivals Celtic.

Richard himself played the captain's role to perfection, coming upfield in the 105th minute to sneak in between goalkeeper Pat Bonner and full-back Chris Morris to stab home a dramatic winner. 'I enjoyed that one. But then I enjoy every goal I score,' says Richard.

However, he is self-critical enough to chastise himself for not scoring more. He netted nine League goals in his first two seasons with Rangers, but none in '89-90. 'I get a few, but I miss more than I should. I get into a lot of good positions without taking full advantage.'

His first goal for Scotland was against Canada in the summer tour of 1983. But apart from the infamous 'rubber watch' goal in Cyprus, the one he enjoyed most was the winner in the 1-0 victory over England at Hampden in May 1985. A header of course, from a Jim Bett cross. The game had been switched to Hampden because there were fears of crowd trouble at Wembley during the Whitsun holiday weekend. That decision allowed 66,489 fans to enjoy a rare moment . . . success over England.

Heads you win. Gough shows typical determination as he towers above Aberdeen giant Brian Irvine to win this aerial joust, watched closely by Dons defender Alex McLeish.

The fact that it meant the Scots had won the inaugural Rous Cup was immaterial. 'Just beating England was enough. I think the fans appreciated the goal more than I did,' says Richard. 'I would like to give them a few more happy moments before I pack it in.' That seems certain . . . and no-one welcomes his return to full fitness more than Scotland coach Andy Roxburgh who sees the Ibrox skipper as a key man in the national plans over the next few years. Gough has now passed on into the 50s in his cap count. But he still claims exclusive membership of the forty-nine and a half cap club!

The future in football is still a long way away as far as he is concerned. But when he does stop playing, I would fully expect him to have a go at being a manager. He has the same hard, ambitious streak as his current boss Graeme Souness. Nuff said.

Richard Gough's international record reads:

1983

Mar.	Switzerland	(h)	2-2
May	Northern Ireland	(h)	0-0
May	Wales	(a)	2-0
June	England	(a)	0-2
June	Canada (3)	(a)	2-0
			3-0
			2-0
Sept.	Uruguay	(h)	2-0
Oct.	Belgium	(h)	1-1
Nov.	East Germany	(a)	1-2
Dec.	Northern Ireland	(a)	0-2

1984

Feb.	Wales	(h)	2-1
May	England	(h)	1-1
June	France	(a)	0-2

1985

Feb.	Spain	(a)	1-1
May	England	(h)	1-0
May	Iceland	(a)	1-0
Sept.	Wales	(a)	1-1
Oct.	East Germany	(h)	0-0
Dec.	Australia	(a)	0-0

1986

Jan.	Israel	(a)	1-0
Mar.	Romania	(h)	3-0
Apr.	England	(a)	1-2
June	Denmark	(W.C.)	0-1
June	West Germany	(W.C.)	1-2
June	Uruguay	(W.C.)	0-0
Sept.	Bulgaria	(h)	0-0
Oct.	Republic of Ireland	(a)	0-0
Nov.	Luxembourg	(h)	3-0

1987

Feb.	Republic of Ireland	(h)	0-1
Apr.	Belgium	(a)	1-4
May	England	(h)	0-0
May	Brazil	(h)	0-2
Sept.	Hungary	(h)	2-0

1988

Feb.	Saudi Arabia	(a)	2-2
Apr.	Spain	(a)	0-0
May	Columbia	(h)	0-0
May	England	(a)	0-1
Oct.	Yugoslavia	(h)	1-0
Dec.	Italy	(a)	0-2

1989

Feb.	Cyprus	(a)	3-2
Mar.	France	(h)	2-0
Apr.	Cyprus	(h)	2-0
Oct.	France	(a)	0-3

1990

Apr.	Argentina	(h)	1-0
Apr.	East Germany	(h)	0-0
May	Egypt	(h)	1-3
May	Poland	(h)	1-1
June	Malta	(a)	1-1
June	Costa Rica	(W.C.)	0 1

1991

1991	USSR	(h)	0-1

Rangers Facts

League Champions (40 times)
1891* 1899 1900 1901 1902 1911 1912 1913 1918 1920 1921 1923 1924
1925 1927 1928 1929 1930 1931 1933 1934 1935 1937 1939 1947 1949
1950 1953 1956 1957 1959 1961 1963 1964 1975 1976 1978 1987 1989
1990.
* In 1891 the Championship was shared with Dumbarton.

Scottish Cup Winners (24 times)
1894 1897 1898 1903 1928 1930 1932 1934 1935 1936 1948 1949 1950
1953 1960 1962 1963 1964 1966 1973 1976 1978 1979 1981.
The Cup was withheld in 1909 after two drawn games with Celtic,
owing to a riot.

Scottish League Cup Winners (17 times)
1947 1949 1961 1962 1964 1965 1971 1976 1978 1979 1982 1984 1985
1987 1988 1989 1991.

European Cup Winners Cup Winners
1972

Scottish Cup-Winning Teams
1947-48 (beat Morton 1-0, after a 1-1 draw)
Brown; Young, Shaw; McColl, Woodburn, Cox; Rutherford,
Thornton, Williamson, Duncanson, Gillick.
1948-49 (beat Clyde 4-1)
Brown; Young, Shaw; McColl, Woodburn, Cox; Waddell,
Duncanson, Thornton, Williamson, Rutherford.
1949-50 (beat East Fife 3-0)
Brown; Young, Shaw; McColl, Woodburn, Cox; Rutherford,
Findlay, Thornton, Duncanson, Rae.

146

1952-53 (beat Aberdeen 1-0, after a 1-1 draw)
Niven; Young, Little; McColl, Woodburn, Pryde; Waddell, Grierson, Simpson, Paton, Hubbard.

1959-60 (beat Kilmarnock 2-0)
Niven; Caldow, Little, McColl, Paterson, Stevenson; Scott, McMillan, Millar, Baird, Wilson.

1961-62 (beat St. Mirren 2-0)
Ritchie; Shearer, Caldow; Davis, McKinnon, Baxter; Henderson, McMillan, Millar, Brand, Wilson.

1962-63 (beat Celtic 3-0 after a 1-1 draw)
Ritchie; Shearer, Provan; Greig, McKinnon, Baxter; Henderson, McMillan, Millar, Brand, Wilson.

1963-64 (beat Dundee 3-1)
Ritchie; Shearer, Provan; Greig, McKinnon, Baxter; Henderson, McLean, Millar, Brand, Wilson.

1965-66 (beat Celtic 1-0 after 0-0 draw)
Ritchie; Johansen, Provan; Greig, McKinnon, Millar; Henderson, Watson, McLean, Johnston, Wilson.

1972-73 (beat Celtic 3-2)
McCloy; Jardine, Mathieson; Greig, Johnstone, MacDonald; McLean, Forsyth, Parlane, Conn, Young. Substitute: Smith (not used).

1975-76 (beat Hearts 3-1)
McCloy; Miller, Greig; Forsyth, Jackson, MacDonald; McKean, Hamilton (Jardine), Henderson, McLean, Johnston. Other Substitute: Parlane (not used).

1977-78 (beat Aberdeen 2-1)
McCloy; Jardine, Greig; Forsyth, Jackson, MacDonald; Russell, Johnstone, Smith, Cooper (Watson). Other Substitute: Robertson (not used).

1978-79 (beat Hibernian 3-2 after 0-0 and 0-0 draws)
McCloy; Jardine, Dawson (Miller); Johnstone, Jackson, Watson; McLean (Smith), Russell, Parlane, MacDonald, Cooper.

1980-81 (beat Dundee United 4-1 after 0-0 draw)
Stewart; Jardine, Dawson; Stevens, Forsyth, Bett; Cooper, Russell, Johnstone, Redford, J. MacDonald. Substitutes: McLean and McAdam (not used).

Scottish League Cup-Winning Teams
1946-47 (beat Aberdeen 4-0)
Brown; Young, Shaw; McColl, Woodburn, Rae; Rutherford, Gillick, Williamson, Thornton, Duncanson.

1948-49 (beat Raith Rovers 2-0)
Brown; Young, Shaw; McColl, Woodburn, Cox; Gillick, Paton, Thornton, Duncanson, Rutherford.
1960-61 (beat Kilmarnock 2-0)
Niven; Shearer, Caldow; Davis, Paterson, Baxter; Scott, McMillan, Millar, Brand, Wilson.
1961-62 (beat Hearts 3-1 after a 1-1 draw)
Ritchie; Shearer, Caldow; Davis, Baillie, Baxter; Scott, McMillan, Millar, Brand, Wilson.
1963-64 (beat Morton 5-0)
Ritchie; Shearer, Provan; Greig, McKinnon, Baxter; Henderson, Willoughby, Forrest, Brand, Watson.
1964-65 (beat Celtic 2-1)
Ritchie; Shearer, Caldow; Greig, McKinnon, Wood; Brand, Millar, Forrest, Baxter, Johnston.
1970-71 (beat Celtic 1-0)
McCloy; Jardine, Miller; Conn, McKinnon, Jackson; Henderson, MacDonald, D. Johnstone, Stein, W. Johnston. Substitute: Fyfe (not used).
1975-76 (beat Celtic 1-0)
Kennedy; Jardine, Greig; Forsyth, Jackson, MacDonald; McLean, Stein, Parlane, Johnstone, Young. Substitutes: McKean and Miller (not used).
1977-78 (beat Celtic 2-1)
Kennedy; Jardine, Greig; Forsyth, Jackson, MacDonald; McLean, Hamilton (Miller), Johnstone, Smith, Cooper (Parlane).
1978-79 (beat Aberdeen 2-1)
McCloy; Jardine, Dawson; Johnstone, Jackson, MacDonald; McLean, Russell, Urquhart (Miller), Smith, Cooper (Parlane).
1981-82 (beat Dundee United 2-1)
Stewart; Jardine, Miller; Stevens, Jackson, Bett; Cooper, Russell, Johnstone, J. MacDonald, Dalziel (Redford). Other Substitute: Mackay (not used).
1983-84 (beat Celtic 3-2)
McCloy; Nicholl, Dawson; McClelland, Paterson, McPherson; Russell, McCoist, Clark (McAdam), J. MacDonald (Burns), Cooper.
1984-85 (beat Dundee United 1-0)
McCloy; Dawson, McClelland; Fraser, Paterson, McPherson; Russell (Prytz), McCoist, Ferguson (Mitchell), Redford, Cooper.
1986-87 (beat Celtic 2-1)
Woods; Nicholl, Munro; Fraser (McFarlane), Dawson, Butcher; Ferguson, McMinn, McCoist (Fleck), Durrant, Cooper.

1987-88 (beat Aberdeen on penalties after 3-3 and a.e.t.)
Walker; Nicholl, Munro; Roberts, Gough, McGregor (Cohen); D.
Ferguson (Francis), Fleck, McCoist, Durrant, Cooper.
1988-89 (beat Aberdeen 3-2)
Woods; Stevens, Brown; Gough, Wilkins, Butcher; Drinkell,
Ferguson, McCoist, N. Cooper, Walters.
1990-91 (beat Celtic 2-1 a.e.t.)
Woods; Stevens, Munro; Gough, Spackman, Brown; Steven,
Hurlock (Huistra), McCoist (Ferguson), Hateley, Walters.

Rangers Scottish League Record

Years	Pld	Won	Lost	Drn	For	Agst	Pts
1890-91	18	13	2	3	58	25	29§
1891-92	22	11	9	2	59	46	24
1892-93	18	12	2	4	41	27	28
1893-94	18	8	6	4	44	30	20
1894-95	18	10	6	2	41	26	22
1895-96	18	11	3	4	57	39	26
1896-97	18	11	4	3	64	30	25
1897-98	18	13	2	3	71	15	29
1898-99	18	18	0	0	79	18	36*
1899-1900	18	15	1	2	69	27	32*
1900-01	20	17	2	1	60	25	35*
1901-02	18	13	3	2	43	29	28*
1902-03	22	12	5	5	56	30	29
1903-04	26	16	4	6	80	33	38
1904-05	26	19	4	3	83	28	41
1905-06	30	15	8	7	58	48	37
1906-07	34	19	8	7	69	33	45
1907-08	34	21	5	8	74	40	50
1908-09	34	19	8	7	91	38	45
1909-10	34	20	8	6	70	35	46
1910-11	34	23	5	6	90	34	52*
1911-12	34	24	7	3	86	34	51*
1912-13	34	24	5	5	76	41	53*
1913-14	38	27	6	5	79	31	59
1914-15	38	23	11	4	74	47	50
1915-16	38	25	7	6	87	39	56
1916-17	38	24	9	5	68	32	53
1917-18	34	25	3	6	66	24	56*

Years	Pld	Won	Lost	Drn	For	Agst	Pts
1918-19	34	26	3	5	86	16	57
1919-20	42	31	2	9	106	25	71*
1920-21	42	35	1	6	91	24	76*
1921-22	42	28	4	10	83	26	66
1922-23	38	23	6	9	67	29	55*
1923-24	38	25	4	9	72	22	59*
1924-25	38	25	3	10	76	26	60*
1925-26	38	19	13	6	79	55	44
1926-27	38	23	5	10	85	41	56*
1927-28	38	26	4	8	109	36	60*
1928-29	38	30	1	7	107	32	67*
1929-30	38	28	6	4	94	32	60*
1930-31	38	27	5	6	96	29	60*
1931-32	38	28	5	5	118	42	61
1932-33	38	26	2	10	113	43	62*
1933-34	38	30	2	6	118	41	66*
1934-35	38	25	8	5	96	46	55*
1935-36	38	27	4	7	110	43	61
1936-37	38	26	3	9	88	32	61*
1937-38	38	18	7	13	75	49	49
1938-39	38	25	4	9	112	55	59*
1946-47	30	21	5	4	76	26	46*
1947-48	30	21	5	4	64	28	46
1948-49	30	20	4	6	63	32	46*
1949-50	30	22	2	6	58	26	50*
1950-51	30	17	9	4	64	37	38
1951-52	30	16	5	9	61	31	41
1952-53	30	18	5	7	80	39	43*
1953-54	30	13	9	8	56	35	34
1954-55	30	19	8	3	67	33	41
1955-56	34	22	4	8	85	27	52*
1956-57	34	26	5	3	96	48	55*
1957-58	34	22	7	5	89	49	49
1958-59	34	21	5	8	92	51	50*
1959-60	34	17	9	8	72	38	42
1960-61	34	23	6	5	88	46	51*
1961-62	34	22	5	7	84	31	51
1962-63	34	25	2	7	94	28	57*
1963-64	34	25	4	5	85	31	55*
1964-65	34	18	8	8	78	35	44

Years	Pld	Won	Lost	Drn	For	Agst	Pts
1965-66	34	25	4	5	91	29	55
1966-67	34	24	3	7	92	31	55
1967-68	34	28	1	5	93	34	61
1968-69	34	21	6	7	81	32	49
1969-70	34	19	8	7	67	40	45
1970-71	34	16	9	9	58	34	41
1971-72	34	21	11	2	71	38	44
1972-73	34	26	4	4	74	30	56
1973-74	34	21	7	6	67	34	48
1974-75	34	25	3	6	86	33	56*
1975-76	36	23	5	8	60	24	54*
1976-77	36	18	8	10	62	37	46
1977-78	36	24	5	7	76	39	55*
1978-79	36	18	9	9	52	35	45
1979-80	36	15	14	7	50	46	37
1980-81	36	16	8	12	60	32	44
1981-82	36	16	9	11	57	45	43
1982-83	36	13	11	12	52	41	38
1983-84	36	15	9	12	53	41	42
1984-85	36	13	11	12	47	38	38
1985-86	36	13	14	9	53	45	35
1986-87	44	31	6	7	85	23	69*
1987-88	44	26	10	8	85	34	60
1988-89	36	26	4	6	62	26	56*
1989-90	36	20	5	11	48	19	51*
	3062	1940	526	596	7008	3179	4474

* Champions   § Joint with Dumbarton